P9-CEN-970

Promise Me, Dad

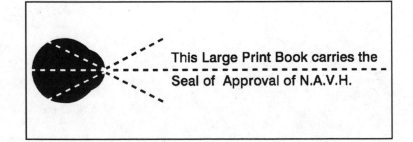

This Large Print Book carries the
Seal of Approval of N.A.V.H.

PROMISE ME, DAD

A YEAR OF HOPE, HARDSHIP, AND PURPOSE

JOE BIDEN

THORNDIKE PRESS
A part of Gale, a Cengage Company

Farmington Hills, Mich • San Francisco • New York • Waterville, Maine
Meriden, Conn • Mason, Ohio • Chicago

GALE
A Cengage Company

Copyright © 2017 by Joe Biden.
Thorndike Press, a part of Gale, a Cengage Company.

ALL RIGHTS RESERVED
Thorndike Press® Large Print Basic.
The text of this Large Print edition is unabridged.
Other aspects of the book may vary from the original edition.
Set in 16 pt. Plantin.

LIBRARY OF CONGRESS CIP DATA ON FILE.
CATALOGUING IN PUBLICATION FOR THIS BOOK
IS AVAILABLE FROM THE LIBRARY OF CONGRESS.

ISBN-13: 978-1-4328-4682-4 (hardcover)
ISBN-10: 1-4328-4682-5 (hardcover)

Published in 2017 by arrangement with Macmillan Publishing Group,
LLC/Flatiron Books

Printed in the United States of America
1 2 3 4 5 6 7 21 20 19 18 17

For Natalie and Hunter

CONTENTS

Rules for Happiness: something to do, someone to love, something to hope for.

— Immanuel Kant

CHAPTER ONE:
BIDEN FAMILY THANKSGIVING

The days were getting shorter, so the light in the sky had started to fall away when the gate to our temporary home swung open and our motorcade edged beyond the fencing that surrounded the United States Naval Observatory in Washington, D.C. We were riding from our official residence at the observatory to Andrews Air Force Base, where my children and grandchildren were already gathering. Jill and I were anxious to be with them for our annual Thanksgiving trip. Family had been an essential escape in the five-and-a-half years I had been vice president; being with them was like flying in the eye of a storm — a reminder of the natural ease and rhythms of our previous life, and of the calm to come when my time in office was done. The job had been an incredible adventure, but there were so many things Jill and I missed from life before the vice presidency. We missed our home in Wilmington. We missed the chance to be alone in a car on a long drive where we could talk with abandon. We missed having command over our own schedule and our own movements. Vacations, holidays, and celebrations with family had become the respites that restored some sense of equilibrium. And the rest of our family seemed to need these breaks as much as Jill and I did.

We had all been together just a few months earlier for our annual summer trip to one of the national parks. But five days of hiking, whitewater rafting, and long, loud dinners in the Tetons had apparently not been enough for the grown-ups. Jill and I were in our cabin packing for departure the last day when there was a knock on the door. It was our son Hunter. He knew Jill and I were going alone to the beach for a four-day retreat. But he wondered if maybe, because he and his wife had some free time, they might tag along. We said, Of course! Within a few minutes our other son, Beau, knocked. His in-laws had agreed to watch the children. Maybe we wouldn't mind it if he and his wife joined us at the beach on Long Island. We said, Of course!

I suspect there are parents who might feel put upon when asked to give up their alone time. I regarded these requests as the fruits of a life well lived: our grown children actually *wanted* to be with us. So we had had another wonderful four days at the beach together in August, but by November there was also a perceptible urgency to this need for togetherness that was a bit disquieting. And I was very mindful of it when Jill and I set out for our yearly escape to Nantucket, for another Biden Family Thanksgiving.

We passed through the gates of the observatory, and I felt our government-required armored limousine make its customary gentle pivot onto Massachusetts Avenue, where local traffic had been halted to clear the path for our journey. I glanced at the squat, standing digital clock at the top of the driveway, as I had maybe a thousand times since we had moved into the official residence. Red numbers glowed, ticking away in metronomic perfection: *5:11:42, 5:11:43, 5:11:44, 5:11:45.* This was the nation's Precise Time, which was generated less than a hundred yards away, by the U.S. Naval Observatory Master Clock. Precise Time — synchronized to the millisecond — had been deemed an operational imperative by the Department of Defense, which had troops and bases in locations around the globe. *5:11:50, 5:11:51, 5:11:52.*

Our limousine was already accelerating out of the turn, with an abrupt force that pushed me back into the soft leather seats. The clock was behind us in a flash, out of sight, but still marking the time as it melted away — *5:11:58, 5:11:59, 5:12:00.* The motorcade arced toward the southeast, down one side of the circle around the observatory, and we could see the lights of the official residence as they flashed through leafless trees. I was happy to say good-bye to the house for a few days. Our departure meant that many of the naval enlisted aides who looked after us were free to spend the entire holiday with their own families.

The procession gained speed once we hit the parkway and our motorcycle escorts nudged aside other travelers. The motorcade traced the southern edge of Washington, within sight of the monuments and public buildings: Arlington National Cemetery, the Lincoln Memorial, the Washington Monument — with the White House in the distance beyond it — the Jefferson Memorial, the United States Capitol. I had served in elective office in this city continuously since 1973, thirty-six years as a senator and six as vice president, but I had not grown indifferent to the beauty and import of these towering landmarks, which were now haloed in a glow of soft light. I still viewed those sturdy marble structures as representatives of our ideals, our hopes, and our dreams.

My working life in Washington had given me a sense of pride and accomplishment from the day I arrived, and that feeling had not dimmed after almost forty-two years. The truth was, on November 25, 2014, I was as excited and energized by my work as I had been at any time in my career, though my current office was, it must be admitted, a truly odd job. There is a strange and singular elasticity to the responsibilities of a vice president. As a strictly constitutional matter, the holder of the office has very little power. He or she is charged with breaking a tie vote in the Senate — which I had not been called to do in nearly six years — and waiting around to take over if the president is somehow disabled. A previous occupant was famously quoted as saying that the office is "not worth a bucket of warm spit." (That's the expurgated version. He did not say "spit.") The actual power of the office is reflective; it depends almost entirely on the trust and confidence of the president.

Barack Obama had handed me big things to run from the beginning of our first term, and once he assigned me to oversee the Recovery Act of 2009, or budget negotiations with Senator Mitch McConnell, or diplomatic relations with Iraq, he did not look over my shoulder. I believe I did my job well enough to earn and keep his trust. He sought my advice as much as ever at the end of 2014, and seemed to value it, which meant there were days when I felt that I had it in my power to help bend the course of history ever so slightly for the better.

And somewhere in the motorcade that evening, as we sped through the streets of Washington, was a car carrying the vice presidential military aide, who was in possession of the "nuclear football," which had to be within my reach at all times. I was one of only a handful of people who had control of the codes that could launch a nuclear strike on almost any target on the planet. So a reminder of the grave responsibilities of the office and the trust reposed in me was there, at all times, twenty-four hours a day, seven days a week.

But in spite of all that, in spite of position and standing, I was incapable of doing the thing I most wanted to do heading into that holiday week: to slow down that Master Clock at the top of my driveway, to make those red ticking numbers hesitate, to give myself, my family, and, most important, my older son, a little extra breathing room. I wanted the power to cheat time.

The Biden tradition of Thanksgiving on Nantucket started as an act of diplomacy, back in 1975. I was a first-term senator and a single father of two boys — Beau was six years old and Hunter just five — and Jill Jacobs and I had started to talk seriously about a future together. Thanksgiving was the first holiday for Jill and me together, and we had too many invitations. My parents wanted us to spend the day with them in Wilmington. Jill's parents wanted us in Willow Grove, Pennsylvania. The parents of my first wife, who had died along with my baby daughter in a car accident a few years earlier, wanted us to bring their grandsons to upstate New York and spend the long weekend with them. No matter which family we chose, we were going to hurt somebody's feelings, which was the last thing either Jill or I wanted to do. I was in my Senate office one day that fall, explaining this predicament to my chief of staff, and he said, "What you need is a nuclear Thanksgiving." Meaning the nuclear family alone. Only Wes Barthelmes was a Boston guy, so what he actually said was "nucleaah Thanksgiving." I wasn't sure what exactly he was trying to say, until he explained it might be easiest on everybody if the four of us — me and Jill, Beau and Hunt — went away alone. He suggested the island of Nantucket, which was an hour by ferry south of Cape Cod. Neither Jill nor I had ever been there, but we decided to go ahead and make an adventure of it.

We filled my Jeep Wagoneer with fifty-seven-cents-a-gallon gas and piled the boys and the dog into the backseat for what was likely to be a six-hour ride to the ferry in Hyannis, Massachusetts. Now, six hours is a long time for two young boys to be trapped in the backseat of a moving car, but Jill was already proving herself a resourceful caregiver. She had picked up every toy catalog and clothing catalog she could find, and when Beau and Hunt started to get restless she tossed the catalogs into the backseat. The three of them spent hours leafing through the pages, and the boys started making and refining their wish lists for Christmas gifts so they would have something to send to Santa Claus, up at the North Pole. Jill told them to take their time and make sure to get it right; there was no rush.

Nantucket turned out to be worth it once we finally got there, eight hours after we left our house in Wilmington. It was chilly on the little island at the end of November, but you could smell the tangy salt air of the Atlantic. The island had emptied for the season, so we had much of the place to ourselves. Most of the restaurants and many of the shops were shuttered. The downtown was tiny, maybe five square blocks, but we spent hours there casing the storefronts and going inside the ones that were open to look around. I told the boys I would buy each of them a single gift on that trip — whatever they wanted, within reason. They took their time to look around. Beau especially liked Murray's Toggery Shop, home of the famous Nantucket Reds; the cotton pants were designed to fade to a soft dusty rose. Hunt fell for the Nobby Clothes Shop, where the owner made a fuss over him. We had Thanksgiving dinner at the Jared Coffin House, a 130-year-old inn built back when Nantucket was a commercial center of the whaling industry, and then we stayed around afterward to sit by the fireplace and play checkers. The next day we had lunch at a restaurant called the Brotherhood of Thieves, went to the little movie house in town, tossed a football on the beach, and drove back into town to watch the annual lighting of the Christmas tree. We took scouting drives around the island, and whenever we passed a radio transmission tower with a big red light on top I'd warn the boys to get down in the backseat so the Red-Eyed Monster couldn't see them. We had such a good time that we even went to check out a little saltbox house that stood above the dunes at 'Sconset Beach. The asking price was too rich for a senator's salary in 1975, but the four of us had our picture taken on the porch of the house, beneath a carved wooden sign that read FOREVER WILD. On the drive back to Delaware, I was already thinking about a return trip the next year.

Jill and I got married a year and a half later and our daughter, Ashley, was born four years after that. And time seemed to move faster. Beau and Hunt graduated high school, then college, then law school. Hunt married Kathleen in 1993, and they had three daughters. Beau married Hallie in 2002, and they had a daughter, then a son. Jill and I were no longer just Mom and Dad; we were "Nana" and "Pop." Ashley finished graduate school and married Howard. And every year, even as the family grew, we spent Thanksgiving on Nantucket — or "Nanatucket," as our grandchildren took to calling it, even when they were old enough to know better. The little trip in the Wagoneer grew into a caravan of two or three cars, with grandchildren shifting loyalties among the fleet at rest stops. Then there was the final mad dash to catch the ferry, and hot chocolate or clam chowder for the ride across the water. We had some great years in that span, and we had some lousy years, but whatever was happening, whatever bumps and bruises we were suffering, we put it all aside and celebrated Thanksgiving in Nantucket. The holiday trip was a constant in our grandchildren's lives from the time they were aware, and they made it clear how much it meant to them. Little notes started appearing at our house as early as September, even before the leaves started to change color, all written out in the grandkids' hands: *Two months to Nana-tucket. Five weeks to Nana-tucket.* Some had drawings of the houses we had stayed at, or the beach. *Two weeks to Nana-tucket. Only five days to Nana-tucket.*

The frolics and habits of our earliest visits grew into immutable family traditions: shopping downtown, lunch at the Brotherhood, the trips to the beach with football in hand. We went back to that little saltbox every year to get the family photo under the carved FOREVER WILD sign. Those pictures became a marker of our family's progress, like the lines parents pencil in on the doorframe as a record of growth — first just the four of us, then five, eight, eleven, and after Beau's son, Hunter, was born in 2006 and Ashley's husband, Howard, joined the family a few years later, we were thirteen strong.

The great work product of the Thanksgiving trip, year after year, continued to be the Christmas lists; it was painstaking, deliberate, and serious business. Nobody shirked, and nobody would be hurried in the enterprise. The catalogs usually came out midway through the drive north, somewhere between the Tappan Zee Bridge and Mystic, Connecticut. But that was only the beginning. There were long sessions after dinners, at whatever inn or house we were in. And it might be the night after Thanksgiving before Jill finally closed down the bidding, and *everybody* — children and grown-ups alike — had to present to her their Christmas list, maximum ten items, minimum ten items. I was invariably in trouble with my grandchildren at the close of business. *Pop only has two! Again!*

There was one little hitch in the great Christmas list endeavor, and that was my becoming vice president in 2009. The entire clan flew together to Nantucket that year on Air Force Two, which struck me as a pretty welcome change after all those hours piloting a car up Interstate 95 during one of the busiest travel weeks of the year, and one that I thought would delight the grandkids especially. But it's not much more than an hour in the air from Andrews Air Force Base to Nantucket Memorial Airport — which turns out to be an interval of time wholly insufficient for catalog browsing. So on the flight back, after the vacation was over and that year's Christmas lists were safely in Jill's hands, my grandchildren filed into my private cabin on Air Force Two en masse, from fifteen-year-old Naomi to three-year-old Hunter. They had all talked it over and the finding was unanimous: this new mode of travel just wasn't going to work for them. "Pop," Naomi spoke for the group, "can we drive again next year?"

I suspected the head of my Secret Service detail, in weighing this consideration against security concerns, was not likely to be swayed by the power of the Christmas list argument — no matter how heartfelt.

Everybody in the family knew the drill by November 2014; this trip would mark our sixth flight to Nantucket on Air Force Two. We usually drove out to Andrews in separate cars and met on the tarmac. The rest of the family was already there when Jill and I pulled up after our twenty-five-minute ride to the air base. Our German shepherd jumped out of the car and scurried across the tarmac. No leash. No guide. This was old hat to Champ. He went right up the stairs and onto the plane. The staircase leading to the entry door of Air Force Two is just wide enough for two people, and there are about twenty steps. I kept an eye on Beau as he made his way up the left side of the staircase. My older son was a little thinner than when I had seen him last, but I thought maybe he had regained some of the strength he had lost in his right arm and his right leg a few months earlier. Getting up those stairs was a struggle, but he insisted on doing it himself. He was fine, he kept saying. In fact, I had not heard him complain once since his diagnosis fifteen months earlier. "It's all good," he would say, over and over. "Getting better every day." I was under strict orders never to betray worry in front of *anybody*. "Dad, don't look at me sad," Beau had admonished me once, when he caught me eyeing him. He had been firm: "Dad. Dad! You understand me? Don't look at me like that."

Two hours after we boarded Air Force Two we were at our friend's house on the island, divvying up bedrooms. Primogeniture was family tradition in the matter of accommodations. Jill and I got to pick first, then Beau and Hallie, then Hunt and Kathleen, then Ashley and Howard, and down through the grandchildren. The White House communications team had already claimed one room in the house. A vice president might leave his office, but the office never left a vice president. The communications staff had wired in a secure telephone line for any emergency or international calls, and set up a secure videoconference hookup to the White House Situation Room just in case.

We had dinner that Tuesday night, two days before Thanksgiving, and afterward sat around with the grandchildren, who insisted we all play Mafia, a whodunit game that could be played around the dining room table. After the younger ones went to bed, the rest of us sat around telling old family stories. Beau and Hunt would not let me forget the day, almost forty years earlier, when I made Beau eat an apple covered in sand after he dropped it, despite having been told not to take it to the beach. And remember when Beau and Ashley dangled a drumstick over Hunt's nose so it would be the first thing he saw when he woke from sleeping off the effects of overeating at the

Thanksgiving feast? And remember the first time we jumped the dunes? It was after midnight when Jill and I finally turned in. We were happy. The family was together in a place that had been nothing but a joy to us for almost forty years. But before we went to sleep Jill and I talked about trimming our sails a bit on this trip — maybe slowing the pace of activity on account of Beau, though we knew he would insist that nothing change. "All good," he would say. "All good."

Nobody spoke it aloud, and they didn't have to, but this Thanksgiving felt different, like there was added pressure to just *be* us. We were fastidious about observing our long-standing rituals. We slept in on Wednesday morning and lazed around as always until Nana prodded the group out the door. We drove into town and started the stroll down the same streets and into the same stores we'd visited for almost forty years. Every member of the family was already in search of the perfect prize. As I had *every* year, I still bought one gift for each person. We hit the Nobby Clothes Shop first, as always, and the owner heard we were there, as always. "Where's Hunt?" Sammy yelled, just like he would when my younger son was still a shy eight-year-old and not a grown man with one daughter in college. Then it was off to the watch shop owned by Spyder Wright, a legendary surfer and surfboard designer who had known Beau and Hunt and Ashley since forever; and the Sunken Ship, a souvenir shop the younger children liked best; and Murray's Toggery Shop.

We traveled in a loose pack, with little groups splintering off to go into particular stores. The older grandchildren would take the younger ones in tow. I wanted to stop in at the Hub to get my coffee, and maybe a newspaper. Ashley and Jill wanted to go to Nantucket Cashmere. Champ was on his own to wander with whatever group showed him the most love. We scouted the shops for hours, cell phones buzzing. *You've gotta come check out the . . .* My White House physician, Kevin O'Connor, who had started making the trip with us the year before, would shake his head at the browsing extravaganza. "It's, what? Four or five blocks of stores?" he would say. "I've been here an hour and I've seen the whole place. What are you *doing* all that time?"

But it felt so good to be out in the holiday crowd again, doing something most people take for granted. Our Secret Service detail gave us a wide berth in Nantucket, so there

27

was an illusion of real freedom. For a moment, everything felt all right. Everything seemed normal.

Our progress was slowed by people who wanted to get a handshake or a hug from the vice president of the United States — or a selfie. And I was not the only draw. Beau Biden was already a rising star in Democratic politics. He was just about to finish his second term as attorney general of Delaware and had already stated his intention to run for governor in 2016. His announcement had cleared the field; nobody back home in Delaware was prepared to challenge Beau in the Democratic primary. He was generally regarded as the most popular politician in the state, more popular than even his father. Delawareans saw in him what I did. Beau Biden, at age forty-five, was Joe Biden 2.0. He had all the best of me, but with the bugs and flaws engineered out. And he had Hunt in his corner as a speechwriter and trusted adviser. I was pretty sure Beau could run for president some day and, with his brother's help, he could win. When Barack and I won reelection back in 2012, I had started thinking hard about stepping aside after the second term and shifting the family's focus to

Beau's political future.

I'm not sure when it happened, but somewhere along the way I had begun to look up to my own sons. They were good and honorable men who shared a belief in public service and had acted on it. Hunt spent the summer after his junior year in college as a member of the Jesuit Volunteer Corps teaching English to children in Belize. His first year after college, JVC work took him to Portland, Oregon, where he was in charge of an emergency services center in a disadvantaged neighborhood. His first big job after he graduated Yale Law School was as an executive trainee at a big bank in Wilmington, where he was on a fast track. But he came to me one night after just a few years and said he needed to do something more meaningful, so he left that high-paying position to take a job in government. By Thanksgiving of 2014, Hunt was in his third year as chairman of the board of the World Food Program USA.

Beau had taken a similar path, propelled by his own steely sense of honor and duty. He had volunteered — as a civilian working in the United States Attorney's office — to go to the war zone in Kosovo to help that emerging republic develop its legal system and its courts. He had joined the Delaware

Army National Guard at age thirty-four, and insisted on going with his unit when it was deployed to Iraq five years later. But he had to make a firm commitment to the Pentagon that he would take a leave of absence as attorney general of the state in order to devote his full energies to his responsibilities in Iraq. He readily did that. I can't say I was happy about how he went out of his way to put himself in harm's way again, but I was not surprised. I considered reminding him that he had already served in one field of fire and he might not want to do it again. But I knew him well enough to know what he'd say: "I signed up for this, Dad. I can't let my guys down. It's my duty."

Beau was also determined to be a good father. There was a story that got passed around by my staff, something that happened on one of our earlier Nantucket trips: Beau and his son Hunter were riding back to the house in one of the cars in the motorcade when Beau decided to make a quick stop at Murray's Toggery to pick up a new pair of Nantucket Reds. His wife, Hallie, would joke that Beau was too conservative to actually wear the flamboyant Reds but liked knowing they were in his closet. When Beau's car peeled off from the main motorcade that morning to detour to Murray's, little Hunter yelled out from his car seat in the back, "Hey, driver, you missed your turn!"

"Please stop the car," Beau said to Ethan Rosenzweig, who was driving. Ethan was the dean of admissions at Emory Law in Atlanta, but he liked to do volunteer advance work for us when he had free time during the holidays. Ethan had known Beau a long time, and he could tell Beau was disturbed. "Hey, Beau," Ethan said, "it's no big deal. He didn't mean anything by it." But Beau urged him to pull the car over. He wanted this lesson to register with Hunter. Ethan pulled onto the shoulder and Beau got out and opened the back door so he could talk to his son. "Look, Hunter," Beau said, and he was firm, "that's Ethan, and he's our friend. You never ever address somebody as 'driver.' You never address somebody by the job they do. That's not polite. Okay? You understand? Love you, buddy."

Beau kept to himself our first day in Nantucket. His Secret Service detail had become really good at walling him away. He was easily fatigued and increasingly shy to interact with people. He was losing feeling in his right hand and it wasn't strong enough for

31

a good firm handshake, and he had been wrestling with a condition called aphasia. Radiation and chemotherapy had done some damage to the part of his brain that controlled the ability to name things. Beau retained all his cognitive capabilities, but he was struggling to recall proper nouns. He was working like hell to win back his strength and to reverse the aphasia. He was going to Philadelphia most days for an hour of physical therapy and occupational therapy and then an hour of speech therapy, all above and beyond his regular chemo treatments. Ashley would meet him there to keep him company at the therapy sessions while he did strength and stretching exercises, or went through sheets of pictures, naming objects. Ashley would take him out for food before he headed off for a day's work as attorney general. He meant to prove to everybody that he could handle this and that he was making progress. And I believed him.

The human brain is remarkably agile, and Beau was literally training other areas near his speech centers to take over the naming function. It was slow going, but he never showed frustration. Nobody in the family, or among his friends, or among his staff at the attorney general's office, saw him angry or down. It just took a little patience, and a

few extra words when he couldn't recall
mayor: "You know, that guy who runs the
city." Or *dinner roll:* "Pass the, you know,
the brown thing you put the butter on."

Part of the beauty of the family vacation
in Nantucket was the splendid and enforced
isolation. The trip had been a no-phone
zone all through my years in the Senate. I
did no business unless some dire emergency
arose, so that my children and my grandchildren had me to themselves. But that was
the one tradition that had grown a bit tattered by 2014. As vice president, I was never
entirely free of work, even around Thanksgiving. For instance, I had to peel off from
the trip to town that Wednesday and get
back to the house to take a call on the
secure line from Arseniy Yatsenyuk, the
prime minister of Ukraine, who was anxious
to fill me in on what had happened in Kyiv
that day. I had been in that city just four
days earlier, and things looked perilous. The
movement started by the Revolution of
Dignity, a remarkable people's protest that
happened on a square in Kyiv called the
Maidan Nezalezhnosti, was fraying. Ukrainians seemed about to lose their fight for
democracy and independence. Russian
president Vladimir Putin had used the
instability of the unfolding revolution as an

opportunity to seize by military force a part of Ukraine called Crimea, and he kept the pressure on. He had lately been sending Russian tanks and soldiers across the border to menace other provinces in the eastern part of the country and was threatening to cut off Ukraine's supply of natural gas, which would have badly destabilized the country's already shaky economy. Ukraine's newly elected democratic government was in real danger of crumbling under the weight of Putin's cynical push.

Ukraine's new president and its new prime minister, meanwhile, were having ongoing trust issues. President Petro Poroshenko and Prime Minister Yatsenyuk were from competing parties, and the recent elections had been bruising and divisive. Their constituencies remained more invested in scoring political points than in governing. The Poroshenko and Yatsenyuk factions were wasting energy bickering with one another when they should have been creating institutions and security forces capable of defending against Putin. The Ukrainians had still not formed a workable coalition government at the end of November, six months after Poroshenko assumed the presidency. If they didn't get that done soon it would mean snap elections. And that meant trouble. Putin operatives were sure to pump money into the campaigns of pro-Russia candidates and probably end any hopes for real independence in Ukraine. The European Union and NATO were likely to abandon Ukraine as a hopeless cause and the country would be pulled back into Russia's toxic orbit. The bravery and sacrifice of so many Ukrainian people in the Revolution of Dignity would come to nothing.

I had spent months exchanging phone calls with both Poroshenko and Yatsenyuk, trying to convince them each, separately, to put loyalty to country over loyalty to political party. I had invested two full days in Kyiv the previous week trying to make Poroshenko and Yatsenyuk see the danger of their stubborn unwillingness to work together. I was still working the problem on my way out of Kyiv on November 22, just four days earlier. Yatsenyuk had called me as I was leaving and I invited him to ride to the airport with me. I liked Arseniy. He was smart — a Ph.D. economist — but no cloistered academic. He was a serious young leader who cared deeply that his home country be a functioning democracy with secure borders. The forty-year-old prime minister also had a streak of idealism I appreciated, and in the limousine ride over to the airport I appealed to that part of him. "Look," I told Yatsenyuk, "you have to be with Poroshenko. You have to be a team. You cannot go your separate ways. If new elections are called, it's going to be a disaster. You're going to lose everything. I'm telling you, Arseniy, you've got to step up. You've got to be the big man. You can do this. It's gonna be hard. But you can do it."

When Yatsenyuk reached me on the secure line in Nantucket that afternoon he had big news, and he wanted me to know first. He told me that the rival parties in Ukraine had just formed a new coalition government. He would remain prime minister, but a key Poroshenko ally would be the Speaker of the new Parliament. The two men had also agreed on an agenda going forward. "I'm keeping my commitment to you, Mr. Vice President," he told me.

I felt pretty good at dinner that night, with the thirteen of us at the table, working through the Christmas lists, and knowing that the parties had worked out a new government in Kyiv.

We got up Thanksgiving morning and did our annual Turkey Trot — a ten-mile run (for anybody who felt up to it) to the other side of the island. I rode the route on a bike with some of the grandchildren. We spent part of the day tossing a football around the beach. I showed young Hunter the bluffs where his father and his uncle used to jump off and catch passes when they were about his age. Beau and Hallie and their kids made sure to get some nice pictures of the four of them together on the beach. And we went over to the little saltbox house for our annual photo, but the lot was ringed with yellow police tape. The house was gone, a victim of rising ocean tides that had been washing away three or four feet of the 'Sconset Bluff every year for the past twenty. Bad storm years might take out ten times that in certain places. "Forever Wild" had finally run out of safe ground, and run out of time; it had been swept out into the Atlantic. The only thing left behind was a piece of the foundation.

We went back to town the day after Thanksgiving, making sure to be at the right spot around dusk, to watch the annual lighting of the Nantucket Christmas tree. Beau had proposed to Hallie at the tree lighting in 2001 and they were married at St. Mary's church, in the heart of downtown Nantucket, the next year. Hallie always suspected it was Beau's way of locking them into Biden Family Thanksgivings for all time. And it worked. They were celebrating their twelfth anniversary at the end of the week, and Hallie had never missed a Thanksgiving. Even the year Beau was stationed in Iraq, she insisted we all keep the tradition and go to Nantucket.

While we did our family stroll, I found myself mulling an issue that was beginning to weigh on me. I was getting a lot of questions, from a lot of different quarters, about running for president in 2016. Even President Obama had surprised me by asking directly about my plans at one of our regular lunches a few weeks earlier. He wanted to know if I had thought about all the things I could do if I *didn't* run. I could still have an effect, he assured me. I could set up a foundation or a center for foreign policy. I could even do a few things I had never done before — like make some money. "But have you made up your mind [about running]?" the president asked me, point blank, across the table in a little private space just off the Oval Office. "No, I haven't," was all I could say.

At some point on the streets of Nantucket that day, I brought up the question of 2016 with my two sons. I had a feeling that they didn't want me to make the run, and I said as much. Beau just looked at me. "We've got to talk, Dad," he said. So when we got back to the house that evening the three of us sat down in the kitchen and we talked.

I knew there were plenty of good reasons not to run, and uncertainty about Beau's health was at the top. And I really suspected that my sons, whose judgments I had come to value and rely on, did not want me to put the family through the ordeal of a presidential campaign just now. "Dad, you've got it all wrong," Beau said when we settled down in the kitchen in Nantucket. "You've got to run. I want you to run." Hunter agreed: "*We* want you to run." The three of us talked for an hour. They wanted to know what I was doing to get ready, and when was the right time to announce. There was a strong argument being made by some of my political experts that if I was going to run at all I should announce right away, at the beginning of 2015. But I think the three of us all wanted a little more time to see what happened with Beau. When I decided was not crucial, my sons told me; they just wanted me to know that they were for it. Hunt kept telling me that of all the potential candidates I was the best prepared and best able to lead the country. But it was the conviction and intensity in Beau's voice that caught me off guard. At one point he said it was my obligation to run, my duty. *Duty* was a word Beau Biden did not use lightly.

When we boarded Air Force Two for the trip home that Sunday, everybody seemed happy. The five days had been a success in all ways. Jill had the completed Christmas lists stowed away for safekeeping. It had been a great trip. The two of us — Jill and I — arrived back at the Naval Observatory that afternoon and went up the sweeping central staircase to the second floor to settle into the casual living quarters we used when it was just the two of us. It was a small space, and somewhat cluttered, but it was our little piece of home inside a residence designed largely for public use. We had furnished the sitting room with leather couches that matched the ones in our library in Wilmington, and lined the shelves with our favorite books and family photos. There was a little table off in one corner that served as our dinner table à deux, where we ate by candlelight even in the long light of summer.

I sat down on our couch, in the one place in the house that felt as though it truly belonged to us, to relax and reflect. But there was an image I could not get out of my head. I kept seeing the little "Forever Wild" house, undermined by the powerful indifference of nature and the inevitability of time, no longer able to hold its ground; I could almost hear the sharp crack as its moorings failed, could envision the tide washing in and out, pulling at it relentlessly and remorselessly until it was adrift on the water, then swallowed up by the sea. No Thanksgiving would ever be quite the same. I pulled out my diary and started to write. I did have one big item for my own Christmas list that year, but I was keeping it to myself: *NavObs, November 30, 2014, 7:30 p.m. Just home from Nantucket. I pray we have another year together in 2015. Beau. Beau. Beau. Beau.*

CHAPTER TWO:
HAVE A PURPOSE

When Beau first saw the scans that showed a lesion on his brain, in the summer of 2013, part of his reaction was relief: he finally had an explanation for what had been happening to him. Beau had awakened one morning three years earlier unable to speak and paralyzed on the right side of his body. He was rushed to the hospital, where the initial scan showed a clot in his brain. But the classic stroke symptoms lifted just a few hours after he got to the emergency room, while the doctors were still deciding how best to treat him. "Dad, look," he called to me from a gurney in an examining room, and moved his right arm and leg up and down. It seemed to me like a miracle. My White House physician, Kevin O'Connor, thought Beau had probably suffered something called Todd's paralysis, which is a common aftereffect of brain seizures. Nobody had a definite explanation, but any sign of a clot had disappeared and Beau had no lasting deficits.

Beau was fine for a few years after that, but then he started to get strange feelings and dizziness on some of his longer runs. He thought it might be dehydration, until it got worse. His balance wasn't always steady and he had auditory hallucinations. On some runs the sound of a jet engine bearing down on him was so real and so present, I found out later, that he would sometimes find himself ducking down by the side of the road. He had started to wonder if these were panic attacks or PTSD from his tour in Iraq, or if he was just losing his marbles. So, disconcerting as it was, the outline of a large mass on the left side of his brain did at least reassure him that he was not going crazy.

They saw the tumor on a scan in Chicago, after Beau had another strokelike episode while on vacation with Hunt and their families. We got Beau back to Thomas Jefferson University Hospital in Philadelphia, where the doctors already knew him and where Ashley's husband, Howard, was affiliated as a head and neck surgeon. The neurologists at Jefferson did a battery of tests and scans before presenting us a range of possible diagnoses: from a benign growth;

to lymphoma, which was likely curable; to glioblastoma, which was likely not. When the doctors at Jefferson suggested that we should prepare for the worst, just in case, Beau's first reaction was anger. *Goddammit!* Then we all got to work.

Howard and Kevin O'Connor, whom we all called Doc, got on the phone with experts to get advice about where the best place for treatment was, whatever the diagnosis. Doc was army like Beau, a Delta Force doctor who had been in serious combat. He was almost always calm under pressure, but even he was a bit shaken by the possibility of glioblastoma. When Jill asked him about the best place to go for a glioblastoma, he blurted out, without thinking — because he would not allow himself to believe it could be the worst — "If it's The Monster, it doesn't matter where we go." Jill burst into tears.

Doc was good with Beau, who was still trying to get his bearings in those first few days. Real fear was starting to creep in. Sometimes Beau would grab him when everybody else was out of earshot to get his honest assessment. "Whatever it is, this is bad," he told Beau, "but we're gonna find out what it is. And once we find out what it is, we will have a plan."

"Promise?" Beau asked.

"Promise. You're good. People do survive this, and all the people who do survive this look like you. They're young. They're fit. They're healthy. We will have a plan."

"Thanks, Doc," Beau said. "You know I love the army."

By the time we got Beau down to M. D. Anderson Cancer Center in Houston just a few days later, all the diagnosticians were leaning toward glioblastoma, but they couldn't be sure. It was hard to fathom, looking at Beau — tan and handsome and fit, with an uncharacteristic week's growth of beard — that there could be anything seriously wrong with him. He looked to me to be as healthy and vibrant as he always had, from the time he was a little boy. He could have gone out and run ten miles that day, and he seemed to be firing on all cylinders. The anesthesiologist at Anderson set aside an hour to explain the very complicated and risky surgery he was going to have the next day to remove the tumor and determine if it truly was glioblastoma. Beau waved him off after twenty minutes. "I got it," he said. *Let's get going on this thing!* We found a big neighborhood Italian restaurant in Houston that night, and nobody there would have guessed we were facing a crisis. We ate, and had some laughs, and projected hope. We were all together: Beau and Hallie, Jill and I, Hunt and Kathleen, Ashley and Howard.

Beau was not kidding himself about the enormity of his situation. The newest scan at M. D. Anderson showed a big gray mass in his left temporal lobe, which meant it was likely threaded through areas in the brain that controlled his speech, cognition, and movement. And yet Beau seemed concerned less about himself and his prognosis than about everybody else in the family. He was worried about his wife and his children, his brother and his sister, his mom, and even about me. When they wheeled him into the Brainsuite for the long and arduous surgery, Howard and Doc were with him. Beau grabbed Doc's hand on the way in. "Doc," he said, "promise you're going to take care of Pop."

"You're going to be around to take care of your dad, Beau."

"Seriously, Doc. No matter what happens. Take care of Pop. For real. Promise me. For real."

While Beau was getting settled into the operating room, the rest of us were escorted to the conference room the hospital's patient

46

affairs staff had kindly set aside for us. There was enough room for the Secret Service detail, and I had a secure telephone line. The Anderson team was working hard to preserve our privacy, which we greatly desired, but the passage to our waiting room added a touch of the surreal. We walked through a maze of hallways, every one muted, beige, and seemingly endless. The panels of lights overhead were a sharp fluorescent white. I think the entire family was feeling like we were in a place we had never been, either physically or intellectually. There was a lot of information coming at us, and fast. I kept thinking there was so much I had to learn about this disease. Would I have the time to learn all I had to know? I could feel control slipping away as we followed our guides down the long hallways. There were no windows, no way to sight a horizon, no way to orient to any foreseeable future. Nobody said a word.

We finally got to the conference room and sat down for the long wait ahead of us.

We had been drawn to M. D. Anderson by the reputation of Dr. Raymond Sawaya, a neurosurgeon who was regarded as among the best in the world at a procedure called awake craniotomy. The operation allowed the surgeon to remove the greatest part of a brain tumor without doing damage to speech, cognition, or motor skills. The patient was actually conscious through most of the surgery, naming simple objects drawn on flash cards or in casual conversation with the anesthesiologist, while Dr. Sawaya probed the outlines of the tumor with tiny electrodes. If Beau suddenly couldn't identify a picture of an elephant or a car, felt a loss of strength, or couldn't talk at all, Sawaya knew he could not cut in that spot without doing serious damage. Beau had to be strong enough to endure hours of this very disconcerting procedure. Dr. Sawaya and his anesthesiologist had allowed Howard and Doc O'Connor into the operating room, so they could help to calm Beau. And they apparently kept things light and easy and humorous. "Remember," one of the medical professionals said, "what happens in the Brainsuite stays in the Brainsuite."

While Dr. Sawaya scouted the area around Beau's tumor for places to cut, he also sent a small biopsy to the lab. He needed to wait for lab results before he started excising the tumor. If the cancer turned out to be lymphoma, Sawaya could be more conservative. Lymphoma would melt away under radiation and chemotherapy, whereas a glioblastoma would be almost entirely unaf-

48

fected by even high doses. So if the lab results confirmed glioblastoma, he would work hard to remove as much as he possibly could. Sawaya had more than seventy long-term survivors among the patients he had treated in the previous thirty years, and what separated these survivors from the rest was the amount of tumor removed in the initial surgery. When Dr. Sawaya got 98 percent or more of the tumor, there was a much better chance for the patient to beat the odds. Anything less made a difficult battle that much harder.

We were all drained and mostly silent when Dr. Sawaya came into our private waiting room sometime after one o'clock that afternoon, more than seven hours after Beau reported to the OR. The surgeon was a tall and elegant man, with a slight soft accent from his early life in Syria and Lebanon. His presence and his demeanor were always confident and comforting, and he was obviously pleased with how the surgery had gone. Dr. Sawaya had removed a tumor slightly larger than a golf ball, he explained, and Beau had come through it without a single complication; except for the scar on the left side of his head, he would be as he was before. His speech, his cognition, and his motor skills were unharmed. But the news was not all good. The tumor was slightly diffuse, and Sawaya had not been able to get all of it. He had detected some microscopic cancer cells right against the wall of an artery, and he knew if he tried to cut them out Beau would have been left with serious and irreversible damage. Then the news got worse. Much worse. The lab results, Dr. Sawaya explained, confirmed the medical team's expectations: Beau's tumor was definitely a glioblastoma. Stage IV. I was at the back of the room, toward the corner, when Sawaya delivered the news — and I was glad no one in the family was looking at me. I put my head down and stared at the floor. I felt like I had been knocked down. I reached for my rosary and asked God to give me the strength to handle this.

Beau was awake and alert later that afternoon, and eating solid food that night. The next morning he was out of bed, walking around, and already anxious to get home. But there was a lot to absorb and a lot of decisions still to make. We were now in the hands of M. D. Anderson's preeminent neuro-oncologist, Dr. W. K. Alfred Yung, who would be overseeing Beau's treatment.

Dr. Yung had grown up in Hong Kong but had come to study medicine in the U.S. He had lost his mother and two siblings to cancer and he was himself a cancer survivor, which meant he was a true and committed warrior against this disease *and* somebody who understood what it was like to be in our shoes.

Dr. Yung had all the new pathology reports in hand. Genetic tests on the mass showed that Beau had the worst of the worst; he lacked a key mutation that slowed the growth of the tumor but had two separate mutations that accelerated it. Yung was gentle, but he was honest and straightforward with Beau. "We're going to be laying out an aggressive treatment plan, and I think you can handle it," he said. "You're young and you're healthy. We know those are good prognostic factors. But you're going to be in for a tough fight, Beau. You have a long battle in front of you."

Beau did not ask Dr. Yung for a judgment as to how much time he might have. Nobody in the family asked, either. We had all looked up the standard prognosis for glioblastoma by then. The tumor usually recurred within six or seven months of surgery, and the median life span after the initial diagnosis was twelve to fourteen months. Maybe two in a hundred get to long-term tumor-free remission. But that means some people *do* beat it, we told ourselves. So why not Beau?

We also knew there were extraordinary advances being made in treating glioblastomas, and we knew that Dr. Yung and the team at M. D. Anderson were on the cutting edge of experimental treatments. I was sure I would have access to the other best minds in the field. Experience had taught me that a vice president was likely to be able to convince almost any doctor or medical researcher in the country to take his call. And I was not going to be shy about asking for help and advice. Beau also had a stalwart support system. Hallie was a rock. She would keep their life on track, make sure their children were well and safe. I knew she would have her hand on Beau's back and put high hopes in his ear. Jill would keep a mother's vigilant eye trained on Beau. If something made him uncomfortable or caused him pain, she would know before he said a word and do whatever she had to do to make it better. Ashley would be there at his side during his treatments in Philadelphia, and offered the unconditional love and adoration of a little sister. Hunt was Beau's secret weapon. His mission his whole life had been to protect his brother; and that's what he'd do. Whatever it took. And Beau knew Hunt would be there whenever he needed him. That didn't even need to be said. They'd always been there for each other, from the time they were little boys, and nothing had changed. It just was more intense now. "You know I'd trade places with you if I could, Beau," Hunt had told his brother the day of the surgery. And we all knew he meant that, literally. Hunt would be the last person in the room to help Beau make the hard decisions about which promising but unproven new treatment might be worth the risk. And he would be the one person in whom Beau could confide anything. While Beau was telling me and everybody else in the world he was fine — "All good. I'm all good" — he could tell Hunt the absolute truth about his very real fears.

More important than that, we were all following Beau's lead, taking our cues from him. And Beau was determined to make the fight — odds be damned. "Don't let anybody tell me what the percentages are," he told Hunt and me. "Okay? I'm going to beat this, goddammit. *We're* going to beat this. I don't want to hear anything about percentages."

■ ■ ■ ■

As we were preparing to leave the hospital, just two days after the surgery, Dr. Sawaya swung by Beau's room to wish him luck. Beau gave him a hug, and Dr. Sawaya returned the embrace. The two men had clearly been through something like battle. When Dr. Yung checked in on us a little later, I pulled him aside and asked him a question all fathers must: "What should my son do now? How should he live?"

He said Beau should be positive and hopeful. He should go home and do whatever he was going to do before the diagnosis. I told him Beau had been planning to run for governor of Delaware. "Then tell him to go home and run for governor," he said. "He should live like he's going to live."

I wanted the entire family to hear that, so I gathered everybody in the little hallway outside Beau's room and Dr. Yung explained again that while this would be a difficult fight, there was hope. I think he was looking at Beau when he said it, but the message was intended for all of us. We should not let this disease take over our entire existence. He told Beau to go home and live like he had a future: "Run for governor.

Have a purpose."

Almost every day after that, I found myself acting on that advice — have a purpose. No matter what came at me, I held fast to my own sense of purpose. I held on for dear life. If I lost hold of that and let Beau's battle consume me, I feared, my whole world would collapse. I did not want to let down the country, the Obama administration, my family, myself, or most important, my Beau.

Chapter Three:
Solace

The White House thought it best that I represent the president at the memorial service in New York for one of the two police officers murdered the Saturday before Christmas 2014. The president was with Michelle and his daughters on their annual holiday trip to Hawaii, where he had grown up, and the staff deemed it unwise for him to take an eleven-hour flight straight into a major controversy. I agreed to do the event. I knew I should do it, even though performing these eulogies had always stirred painful memories of my own losses and had taken on a sense of foreboding as well since Beau's diagnosis. So I spent the last few days before Christmas preparing remarks. I knew I had to strike the perfect balance to help start the healing in New York City. The killings of uniformed New York City policemen Rafael Ramos and Wenjian Liu was another in a series of sudden, violent tears in the tattered relationship between cops and the black community. The two men were executed by a lone gunman while sitting quietly in their patrol car in Brooklyn, just doing their job. "They were, quite simply, assassinated — targeted for their uniform," New York City police commissioner Bill Bratton had said in announcing the deaths of the two cops. "They were ambushed and murdered."

News of the senseless act hit in the middle of more than two weeks of growing demonstrations against police brutality in the city. Those protests had been sparked by a grand jury's decision not to indict a policeman who had choked to death a forty-three-year-old African American man named Eric Garner — in spite of the fact that the entire incident was preserved on cell phone video. New York mayor Bill de Blasio had been careful not to criticize the grand jury, but he did make a point of expressing sympathy for the Garner family and for every parent who had to worry about his or her non-white son in any encounter with the cops. The mayor detailed the special precautions he and his wife insisted their mixed-race son observe in his dealings with police: do everything they tell you to do, don't move suddenly, don't reach for your cell phone.

"I've had to worry over the years," the mayor explained. "Is Dante safe each night? . . . And not just from some of the painful realities of crime and violence in some of our neighborhoods but safe from the very people [we] want to have faith in as their protectors." The head of the city's largest police union, Patrick Lynch, immediately accused the mayor of throwing police "under the bus."

When de Blasio got word of the ambush of Ramos and Liu in Brooklyn he rushed to the hospital to comfort their families and friends. The mayor forcefully condemned the killings, and did so without pause, as did President Obama. "Officers who serve and protect our communities risk their own safety for ours every single day and they deserve our respect and gratitude every single day," the president said. "I ask people to reject violence and words that harm, and turn to words that heal — prayer, patient dialogue, and sympathy for the friends and family of the fallen." But things were already getting out of hand.

New York congressman Peter King was visibly distraught when he went on TV just hours after the shooting. Representative King is a reasonable and dedicated public servant, but his anger at the awful murder seemed to have got the better of him. The statements by the president and the mayor were perfunctory and disingenuous, King told one interviewer. It was "time for elected officials to stand by the men and women of law enforcement and end the demeaning of police officers and grand juries," King said, implying that the president and the mayor were part of the problem. Former New York mayor Rudy Giuliani was already, in the first hours after the shooting, being outrageous. And he knew from long experience that a number of press outlets would allow him to speak unchallenged. He asserted that the president had given license to the gunman, who was found to have announced on social media his intention to hunt and kill police officers to avenge Garner and others who had been killed during recent interactions with law enforcement. "We've had four months of propaganda, starting with the president, that everybody should hate the police," Giuliani said, a statement both mean-spirited and demonstrably false. Patrick Lynch was even more dramatic. "There's blood on many hands tonight," he said. He blamed all "those that incited violence on the streets under the guise of protest that tried to tear down what NYPD officers did every day. . . . That blood on the hands starts at the steps of city hall, in the office of the mayor."

Giuliani, Lynch, and a handful of others just kept clawing away in the days after the shooting, unmoved by the many generous New Yorkers who had marched against the unjustified death of Eric Garner but also showed up to pay their respects at a make-shift sidewalk memorial for Officers Ramos and Liu — including Garner's own daughter, who arrived to offer the sympathy of one who truly understood. "I had to come out and let their family know that we stand with them," said twenty-two-year-old Emerald Snipes-Garner, rising to the occasion in a way that should have made the entire country proud, "and I'm going to send my prayers and condolences to all the families who are suffering through this tragedy."

By the time I headed to New York for Officer Ramos's funeral on Saturday, December 27, the city felt like it was on a hair trigger. Hundreds of New Yorkers had refused to suspend their demonstrations as a show of respect for the slain policemen. "We mean no disrespect to anybody," said an organizer of one march, beneath a sign that read RACIST POLICE TERROR. "But we're out here to say it's ridiculous, it's outrageous, it's insulting for anybody to ask us to stop these protests." At the same time, police from around the country had traveled to New York to attend Rafael Ramos's memorial in a show of support for a brother officer and his comrades. As many as twenty-five thousand law enforcement officers were gathering in Queens to attend the funeral, and some local politicians kept telling them that they were in "grave danger" these days and had "targets on their backs." Folks like Lynch and Giuliani were still trying to convince them and everyone else that Mayor de Blasio and President Obama were the problem.

Mayor de Blasio seemed happy that it was me representing the administration because he knew I had a close relationship with the police and the civil rights community. The mayor had called me a few days after the shootings to ask for some help in dealing with the growing chasm of distrust between law enforcement and the black community. Truth was, as impossible as the situation might appear, I believed I knew a way across the divide. I had crossed it before, at home in Delaware as well as around the country. There were always the demagogues on both sides of the issue, that was inevitable, but I knew they didn't represent the vast majority of the people. I have always believed the problem was solvable — because the problem was obvious. There were real, legitimate fears on both sides. And if the problem is fear, the answer is knowledge. Each side has to be willing to try to understand the concerns of the other.

That's why, way back in the late eighties, when the crime rate exploded, I began to pursue a new — but in fact a very old — concept of policing. That was getting cops back walking the street so they'll know the shopkeepers, know the kids in the neighborhood, know the neighborhood. And getting the neighborhood to know the cops and to trust them. We had moved away from that concept — the new model was a lone cop riding around in a police cruiser instead of walking the beat — and the best criminologists were advocating the old idea with a new name: community policing. But it was a hard fight to get it done in the late eighties and early nineties because the national Republican Party had begun to talk about devolution of power: anything local should be paid for with local funds, not federal taxes. And they argued that crime was uniquely local. I had to remind my colleagues that most local crime was caused by the drug epidemic, and drugs were a federal responsibility. It took some time, but I finally got real funding written into the crime bill I authored in 1994 that provided an additional one hundred thousand local cops. And it worked.

Violent crime dropped precipitously, from almost 2 million incidents in 1994 to 1.4 million in 2000. The murder rate nationwide was cut nearly in half. Relations between the police and the black community, while far from perfect, were much improved. But community policing became a victim of its own success. As crime went down, so too did public pressure to focus on policing. Polling data indicated that crime had dropped way down the list from being the number-one problem Americans wanted their government to fix. That meant that when the Bush administration came into office and renewed the ideological call for devolution of power, there was no longer much pushback on their argument that crime was a strictly local matter. Why spend federal money on local police when you can lower taxes on the wealthy instead?

I sometimes felt like a lonely voice in those years, constantly warning people that making communities safe is like cutting grass. You cut your grass on a beautiful summer weekend and it looks great. You let it go for a week, it gets a little ragged. You let it go for a month, it looks bad. You let it go for the summer, you've got a disaster on your hands.

And that's exactly what happened. There were fewer and fewer cops on the beat, with the predictable consequence of increasingly strained relations between the police and the black community. Police weren't getting out of their cars to meet people as much anymore. They were more and more riding around alone, understandably fearful in the toughest neighborhoods, sometimes in surplus military and paramilitary equipment that made them look like invaders instead of protectors. Dramatic footage of high-profile deaths was constantly on television news and spread like wildfire through social media. As awful stories of Eric Garner in New York, Michael Brown in Ferguson, twelve-year-old Tamir Rice in Cleveland, and Officers Ramos and Liu took over the headlines, it grew harder and harder for either side to acknowledge the basic humanity of the other.

The local cop in the squad car would look at the fifteen-year-old boy in a hoodie on a street corner as a criminal in training, instead of as an aspiring writer who might one day be the poet laureate and deserved a chance. The people in the neighborhood saw the policewoman in her car as a threat, instead of as a mom who coached basketball, taught Sunday school class, wanted more than anything in the world to make it home safely to tuck in her three children, and deserved the right to do so.

I thought it was time to get back to the proven policy of investing in more and better-trained men and women on the beat. I told Mayor de Blasio a few days before the Ramos funeral that I would send him the statistics on community policing and sit with him after the first of the year, after the latest firestorm calmed down, if he wanted to talk it through.

President Obama had been working hard to find ways to improve relations between the police and *all* the communities they served, and had developed very specific policy proposals. But there were too many people invested in scoring political points instead of solving the problem, and attacks on the president by people like Lynch and Giuliani made it almost impossible for him to get a fair hearing.

I had been around long enough to know that good policy was always necessary but rarely sufficient. I had worked long and hard over the years to build personal relationships and gain the trust of both sides so that

65

I could reason with both the police and the community in the most inflamed of circumstances. I had always tried to understand everybody's perspective. "You are the only one who can do this, Joe," our secretary of education, Arne Duncan, told me just after the shooting in New York. "You are respected by both communities." Arne may have given me more credit than I deserved, but his encouragement served as a reminder of what drew me to public service and why I had stayed in it for so long. I have come to believe that the first duty of a public servant is to help bring people together, especially in crisis, especially across difficult divides, to show respect for *everybody* at the table, and to help find a safe way forward. After forty-five years in office, that basic conviction still gave me purpose.

I was making last-minute edits and notations on my prepared remarks as Jill and I flew on Air Force Two from Washington to New York on that sparkling winter morning. Funerals are for the living, I have always believed, and the job of the eulogist is to acknowledge the enormity of the loss they have just suffered and to help them appreciate that the legacy and accomplishments of their loved one have not died with them. I also try hard to assure them that they are not alone. I had to do that for the Ramos family first, but also for the larger police family that would be watching Officer Ramos's memorial service. Police in the city — and around the country — were angry and grieving. Some were also genuinely hurt that so many people seemed to have turned against them. They needed to be reminded that their service was worthy of our honor and respect. Being a cop is not just what these men and women do, I have always said, it is who they are. I could pick out the sort of classmate who would become a cop when I was still in grade school. They were the person who came to your defense when you got jumped in the neighborhood. When you were being bullied, they stepped in. They wanted to protect other people.

I ran my pen along the words on the paper, making little notes about where to pause and what words to emphasize: "In my experience, and I'm sure this applies to every man and woman in uniform within the sound of my voice, every cop joins the force for the same underlying reason: You felt a sense of obligation. You thought you could help. That's the single element, I think, that runs through all of American law enforcement. When events like this occur, the nation is always reminded of your bravery." I was reading through the speech for a final time when we pulled up to Christ Tabernacle Church in Queens at around nine thirty that Saturday morning. The church looked like a converted storefront and was way too small to accommodate the massive crowd waiting outside. More than twenty thousand men and women, almost all of them in uniform, stood quietly in the surrounding streets and parking lots preparing to watch a satellite feed of the services on the big screen hoisted above.

I exited the car into a bracing winter day and could feel the tension in the air. The temperature was rising toward forty, but it still felt cold, and the sky was a sharp crystalline blue that looked like it could crack into a thousand pieces. Our escorts hustled Jill and me inside the sanctuary and steered us down to our seats in the front row, while I tried to adjust my eyes to the dark interior of the evangelical church. The church had been Rafael Ramos's spiritual home and his guide; he was just hours away from graduation from a volunteer chaplain program when he was killed. When I sat down, my knees were almost touching Officer Ramos's casket, which sat on the bier in front of the stage. The other main speakers

68

were already in their seats; the mayor was there, along with Police Commissioner Bratton and Governor Andrew Cuomo. I felt a slight pang when I saw the governor. He reminded me of Beau, who was in the final days of his term as Delaware's chief law enforcement officer. From his days as assistant U.S. attorney in Philadelphia to his job as attorney general in Delaware, Beau had worked on crime issues every day and had also worked hard to improve relations between the police and the community so that these deadly tragedies could be avoided. He very much wanted to travel with me, to pay his respects, but his physical disabilities were really beginning to take a toll. "I'm going to wait until I get better, Dad," he said.

I was called up to the podium to speak first, and as I took the stage the audience sat in reserved silence. I turned first to offer a simple and straightforward expression of condolence from my own family to the Ramos family and was brought up short by the image of the victim's two teenage sons sitting in front of me. They were much too young to have lost a parent. I found myself unable to shift my gaze from the boys. It was almost like I was watching young Beau and Hunt sitting in those chairs, staring up at me, and it reminded me of the devastation they had faced in losing their mother and what it meant to me that they had survived. It reminded me also that however high the political and public stakes, my mission here in New York was, at its heart, a personal one. If I allowed the Ramoses' loss to be overshadowed by the politics of the day, I would fail. "What handsome boys," I said, already off my carefully prepared text. "I remember a similar occasion a long time ago.

"Mom, I assure you," I told Maritza Ramos, "those boys will get through all of this. I'm sure I speak for the whole nation when I say to you that our hearts ache for you. I know from personal experience there is little anyone can say or do at this moment to ease the pain, that sense of loss, that sense of loneliness. But I do hope you take some solace in the fact that, as reported by the press, there are over twenty-five thousand — twenty-five thousand — members of the same fraternity and sorority as your husband who stand, and will stand, with you, the rest of your life. And they will. It's an uncommon fraternity."

The writer who helped me on this speech was the son of a retired New York City police detective who had taken the time to

70

understand Rafael's life and what his sons meant to him. "Justin and Jayden," I told them, "he was so, so very proud of you, and just know, as hard as it is for you to believe, he will be part of your life, the entirety of your life." Then I found myself turning to the young widow and making a guarantee I had made to countless other survivors over the years. "I also know from experience that the time will come, the time will come, when Rafael's memory will bring a smile to your lips before it brings a tear to your eyes. That's when you know — it's going to be okay. I know it's hard to believe it will happen, but I promise you, I promise you it will happen. And my prayer for you is that it will come sooner rather than later."

I was off script by then, but not at all uncertain about what I meant to say: "I've spoken to too many funerals for too many peace officers, too many funerals for brave women and men who keep us safe. And watched their families grieve. And unfortunately, it's only when a tragedy like this occurs that all their friends, neighbors, and people who didn't even know them become aware of and reminded of the sacrifices that they make every single, solitary day to make our lives better. . . . Police officers and police families are a different breed. Thank

God for them. Thank God for them.

"Your husband, Mrs. Ramos, and his partner, they were a part of New York's Finest. And that's not an idle phrase. This is probably the finest police department in the world. The finest police department in the world. They earned that phrase. . . .

"When you patrol the streets of New York you circle the earth. The three-story walkups, the apartment towers, the aromas of a million kitchens continuing a thousand traditions. Streets full of silence and streets bursting with a hundred languages — whispering. Shouting. Laughing. Crying. In every neighborhood of this most alive of all cities — this chaotic miracle that stands as a beacon for the world.

"The assassin's bullet targeted not just two officers, not just a uniform. It targeted this city. A city where the son of Chinese immigrants shares the patrol with a Hispanic minister in training."

And I reminded everybody listening that this greatest and most diverse of American cities had helped to nurture a young college student named Barack Obama. My friend the president learned something here in New York that remained a cornerstone of his career in government service: "There is not a black America and a white America

72

and Latino America and Asian America," he had said in the speech that introduced him to the country ten years earlier. "There's the United States of America."

The morning was even brighter when Jill and I were led out of Christ Tabernacle and across the street to await the move of Rafael Ramos's casket onto the thronging avenue and into the hearse. The sun was glinting off the top of the lead car, but it felt as if the day itself had softened. I found myself standing in a group of dignitaries that included Representative King and, at my right shoulder, Rudy Giuliani. Giuliani could not resist taking a backhand shot at the president. "At least somebody in the administration gets it," he told me.

I held my tongue. "The president gets it" was all I said, though it didn't seem to register.

The bagpipers played. A group of New York Police helicopters flew overhead in formation. And the honor guard walked the flag-draped coffin toward the hearse's open back door. I could see Jayden and Justin across the street from me, their dark suits buttoned against the cold, their brows furrowed, holding their mother's hands. All the rest of us could do was stand in silence, with

73

hands over hearts. When the coffin was finally loaded and the flag presented to the family, the hearse started for the cemetery. After it had made the turn off the avenue, I began hearing voices from within the crowd of cops lining the street: "Joe!" "Hey, Joe!" Nobody yelled, "Mr. Vice President!" It was "Joe!" *"Hey, Joe!"* like they knew me. Men and women in uniform began coming over to shake my hand and I felt an occasional tug as the motorcycle cops riding by reached down to touch my hand. The first part of the day was done, but not the hardest part.

Jill and I had one more stop to make before we left New York — one I had insisted on, though I knew there would be nothing easy about it. We had a forty-five-minute drive down to the Gravesend area of Brooklyn, to visit the family of Wenjian Liu, the other murdered police officer. He was just thirty-two years old, a newlywed who had bought a house big enough for his parents to live with him and his new bride. Liu's funeral had been delayed because so many of his relatives in China were still trying to get proper travel documents to make the trip to New York, and I knew I would be unable to return for that service. I wanted to pay my respects, at the very least, but as our motorcade skirted Jamaica Bay,

Brighton Beach, and Coney Island, I was certain there was much more I could offer the Liu family.

I have found over the years that, although it brought back my own vivid memories of sad times, my presence almost always brought some solace to people who have suffered sudden and unexpected loss. Not because I am possessed of any special power, but because my story precedes me: I was a newly elected thirty-year-old United States senator, excited to be down in Washington interviewing staff, when I got the call that my wife and eighteen-month-old daughter had died in a car accident while out shopping the week before Christmas. Beau and Hunt had been in the car, too. They pulled through without permanent damage, but not before spending weeks in the hospital. The pain had seemed unbearable in the beginning, and it took me a long time to heal, but I did survive the punishing ordeal. I made it through, with a lot of support, and reconstructed my life and my family. When I talk to people in mourning, they know I speak from experience. They know I have a sense of the depth of their pain.

One thing I have grown especially attuned to over the years is just how many people are quietly and uncomplainingly suffering psychic and emotional pain at any given time. Consider the simple fact that as I sped along a highway at the far edge of America in the last few days of 2014, more than two and a half million of our fellow citizens had perished in that single year. A fifth of those people had died of cancer, which meant they had likely suffered long, harrowing, and painful deaths as their families looked on feeling helpless. A population twice the size of my hometown of Wilmington had died in some form of accident. Here and healthy one day; gone forever the next. Almost forty-three thousand adults and teenagers had committed suicide in 2014. Alcohol-related deaths numbered more than thirty thousand; drug-related deaths were at nearly fifty thousand and climbing every year. The majority of drug deaths were men and women under forty. Gun deaths were close to thirty-four thousand in 2014, and two-thirds of those were suicides or accidents. As in most years, nearly 1 percent of our fellow citizens had died. The simple statistics tell so little of the real and complicated human story. These were not mere numbers. These were people like Rafael Ramos, whose death had blown a gaping hole in the lives of the family I had just seen, and who would never have the chance to use his new chaplaincy to make hundreds of lives, if not thousands, a little better.

Consider that almost everybody who died had left behind at least one or two people who were deeply and profoundly wounded by the loss; some left a dozen bereft, others a score. It amazes me how many people there are who endure and live with devastating loss with nowhere near the support I have had, who get up every single day, put one foot in front of the other, and simply carry on. They continue to do their jobs, run their daily errands, and raise their children as single parents — and often without complaint. There is an army of these soldiers. By my estimation, at any given moment, one in ten people in our country is suffering some serious degree of torment because of a recent loss, and I'm not just citing statistics again. I see them at the rope lines at any political event I do, standing there, with something behind their eyes that is almost pleading. *Please, please, help me.* It's always more practical to simply pass them by, to avoid any extraneous personal entanglements, to not get thrown off the schedule. We all spend so much time on the move, racing to keep up with the imperatives of modern life and personal ambition. So I try to be mindful, at all times, of what a difference a small human gesture can make to people in need. What does it really cost to take a moment to look someone in the eye, to give him a hug, to let her know, *I get it. You're not alone?*

There were nine officers in dress uniform standing guard outside the Liu house when we arrived. The NYPD had also called in a translator because Liu's parents, though they had come from China twenty years earlier, were not comfortable speaking English and preferred to speak in their native Cantonese. They had depended on their son. Wenjian had been twelve when the family arrived, so he had been well schooled in the English language and American culture. He grew up an only child helping his parents navigate their new world, and he was still doing it at the time of his death. He had even brought his parents along on his honeymoon three months earlier.

The younger Liu was an immigrant success story. The first souvenir he bought in New York was a sticker of the Statue of Liberty. He had gone to college and studied accounting, but after the attack on the World Trade Center on September 11, 2001, he was determined to become a police officer. He was newly married at the time of his death, a homeowner, and a seven-year veteran of the police department, doing the job he most wanted to do. But it wasn't just about what he had accomplished, but what he looked forward to doing. Wenjian Liu was the future of that family, and he and his new wife were already talking about having children. His sons and daughters would have started on solid ground, with a father who could help them navigate toward whatever they wanted in life, and I could sense that lost future when I walked up the little outdoor steps and into his home.

About twenty of his extended family members were seated in the kitchen so that his wife and parents could comfortably receive Jill and me in the living room. Liu's father gave me a hug when we entered and touched my face. He was a small wiry man who was trying hard to be brave. "Thank you," he said, over and over, while his wife kept her distance and bowed politely. "Thank you," Wei Tang Liu said, remaining close. "Thank you. Thank you."

Officer Liu's wife, Pei Xia Chen, was so young and so beautiful. She went by "Sanny." English was not her first language, but she was fluent, so she did the speaking for the family. Her welcome was quiet and halting. I could tell she was not only distraught at the death of the man she called the love of her life, her best friend, and her hero, but also a little intimidated to have the vice president of the United States and his wife in her home. But it didn't take long for her to relax, and soon she told us she had something she would like to show us in the bedroom she had shared with her husband. Jill was always shy to invade people's personal spaces, but Sanny insisted. She took us by the hand and the three of us went into the bedroom.

What Sanny wanted us to see was a picture of the two of them outside, embracing, on their wedding day three months earlier. I was struck by the size of the portrait, how happy they both looked, how proud they must have been to hang it in plain sight, and how sad she was now while looking at it. I had been there, right where she was. I could remember vividly, after my wife Neilia died, not being able to open the closet door of the bedroom we shared. I could recall the anguish of smelling her scent on the pillows and looking at the empty spot on the bathroom sink where her toothbrush had been. I wasn't able to stay in that bedroom; I sold my house and got out. And I found myself wondering how Sanny would handle it, and sorry that she had to.

I pulled her aside to offer some counsel about what she was facing. I shared some of the best advice I got after Neilia's death, from the most unexpected sources. There was a former governor of New Jersey who called me out of the blue to tell me about losing his wife. For the longest time he thought things were never, ever going to get better. Six months after his wife died, he would think of her and he would be just as miserable as the day he got the news. He was terrified it would never get better, and he knew I was probably feeling the same way. He told me to get a calendar, and every night, before I went to bed, put down a number on that day's date. One is as bad as the day you heard the news, he said, and ten is the best day of your life. He told me not to expect any tens, and he said don't spend any time looking at that calendar, but mark it every day. After about six months, put it on graph paper and chart it. What he promised me turned out to be true: the down days were still just as bad, but they got farther and farther apart over time.

I also told Sanny in more detail what I try to tell everybody: There will come a time when you'll go riding by a field that you both loved, or see a flower, or smell the fragrance of his suit when he took it off and hung it in the closet, or you'll hear a song, or you'll look at the way someone walks, and it will all come back. But someday down the line, God knows when, you'll realize it doesn't make you want to cry. It makes you smile. "The time will come when the memory will bring a smile to your lips," I would tell everyone in that situation, "before it brings a tear to your eyes." That *will* happen, I assured her. And that is when you know that you've turned a corner.

The last thing I did before we left the bedroom was to give her my private phone number. "Right now, you know, everyone is going to be there for you," I explained. "Everyone will surround you with love and you'll be busy and have things to keep your mind off the worst. And then in six weeks, or maybe twelve weeks, everybody else's life is going to start to get back to normal. But your life isn't going to be normal again. As a matter of fact, as you probably understand already, it's going to get harder for you. And after a while you're going to start to feel guilty because you're going to be going to the same people constantly for help, or just to talk. And as their lives get back to normal, you are going to start to worry about leaning on them too much. There might come a time when you think, I'm asking too much. I've got to stop complaining.

"So when you're down and you feel guilty for burdening your family and friends," I said, "pick up the phone and call me." I got the sense she didn't quite believe I was entirely sincere. But I was. I have a long list of strangers who have my private number, and an invitation to call, and many of them do. "Just call me when you want to talk," I told her. "Sometimes it's easier to pour your heart out to somebody you don't know well, but you know they know. You know they've been through it. Just pick up the phone and call me."

We were at the little house in Gravesend for almost an hour, and near the end of the visit I started to notice that Wenjian Liu's father had rarely left my side. Occasionally he would lean into me so that his shoulder touched my arm. "Thank you," he kept saying. "Thank you. Thank you." I did not pull away, but leaned in so that he could feel me there. When our advance team came to pull us out of the house, Wei Tang Liu insisted on accompanying me back outside, into the cold, wearing nothing but a cotton turtleneck, slacks, and open sandals over his socks. He seemed oblivious to the cold and remained right at my shoulder, as if he were desperately trying to convey something I needed to know. Wei Tang would call the day he lost his only son the saddest in his life. Wenjian had been an exemplar of Confucian filial piety, he would tell other mourners, a respectful, obedient, and caring son. He would tell people how his son always insisted on taking him to the doctor whenever he felt sick, or stopped by the garment factory to help him finish his piecework before driving him home, or called him every day before he finished his shift to assure him that he was safe and coming home. "You can stop worrying now," Officer Liu would tell his father.

But I didn't know any of that at the time. He didn't have the English to express it to me, and I didn't have the Cantonese to understand him. When Wei Tang gave me a final hug in front of his house, in front of the line of policemen standing guard, he held on to me tightly, for a long time, as if he could not bear to let me go. We stood there for a long while, embracing on the little sidewalk in front of the house where he had lived with his only son, just two fathers. I understood all that he wanted me to know — or thought I did.

CHAPTER FOUR:
TRUST

The call came right on schedule, at twelve thirty in the afternoon on the first Monday of the New Year, 2015: "Excuse me, sir, the president is ready for you." I grabbed my small card with notes about the issues I wanted to discuss that day and set off on the forty-five-second walk from my office to his, for our weekly private lunch. Sometimes on the walk down I would think about the first time Barack Obama and I ever talked about having a meal together. It was exactly ten years earlier, back when Obama was a forty-three-year-old newly elected senator just trying to get his bearings in Washington; he wanted to be on the Foreign Relations Committee. I was the top Democrat on the committee, and senior enough that I could determine who got an open seat, so he asked to come see me.

It was clear Senator Obama would be a great asset on the committee. He seemed to

85

have a breadth and depth of intellect, a willingness to work hard, and a sense of America's role in the world — both the possibilities and the limitations — that was similar to my own. Beyond that, his speech at John Kerry's Democratic National Convention the previous summer had really impressed me, as it had everyone who heard it. When he talked of the "true genius of America, a faith in simple dreams, an insistence on small miracles," he sounded like a guy who sang from the same hymn-book I did. "People don't expect government to solve all their problems. But they sense, deep in their bones, that with just a slight change in priorities, we can make sure that every child in America has a decent shot at life, and that the doors of opportunity remain open to all."

When Barack came to my office to pay his respects on that cold winter day ten years earlier, I told him I'd be happy to have him on the committee and I would make sure it happened. We didn't have much time to talk, and I suggested we meet again, get to know each other a little better. I knew his family was still back in Chicago and he was commuting, as I was, so I told him if he ever wanted to grab dinner together some night I'd be happy to do that. I could stay down after Senate business was done and we could go to a local Italian restaurant just off the Hill. "Nothing fancy," I said.

"Oh, we can go to a nice place," he said, explaining that his book royalties had set him up just fine. "I can afford it."

I can afford it" rang in my ears as a strange comment, bordering on arrogant. It only occurred to me later, as I got to know him well, that Barack was not the sort to talk about what he could afford, and that he might have been offended that I had taken him for a man of limited resources. Just as it probably did not occur to Barack at the time that I *am* a man of limited resources. We never did have that dinner, but he and I had an awful lot of lunches in the years after that.

Barack Obama first called me about being considered as his running mate in June 2008, not long after he had secured enough delegates for the nomination. I was riding home to Wilmington on the train when my phone rang. He asked my permission to vet me, and I said no. "I'll help you any way I can," I told him, "but I don't want to be vice president." I obviously didn't say this lightly. I was honored to be asked, but I had been a United States senator for thirty-five years, a job I loved, in an institution I revered. I had gained respect as a formidable legislator and had seniority. I was my own man, and I enjoyed what I was doing. I also believed I could make more significant contributions as chairman of the Foreign Relations Committee than I could as vice president.

He insisted that this was not just an exercise and gave me the impression that I was already his leading candidate. "This is real," he said. "But I need an answer now."

"Then the answer is no."

"Do me a favor, Joe. Go home and talk it over with the family first."

I agreed to do that, and when I hung up I called Jill and asked her to call a family meeting. The five of us sat down that evening to talk.

My family's response surprised me. They were all for it. Beau and Hunt argued that I could help Obama win key states like Pennsylvania, Ohio, and Florida, and my foreign policy experience would help the ticket.

Jill was actually relieved by Barack's call. She had been afraid, based on all the well-placed Democrats suggesting it to her, that Obama was going to recruit me to be his secretary of state and I'd live the next four years on airplanes and in foreign capitals. Being vice president would be a new challenge for the entire family, she said. There was also something appealing to Jill about having the vice president's official residence as a base in Washington, which would mean we would have one home just a few minutes away from Hunt and his three daughters, and another a few minutes from Beau and his two children. It would eliminate the four-hour commute I had been making every day the Senate was in session for the last thirty-five years and it would give me more access to my grandchildren.

The other compelling argument was this: even if my participation was just a footnote, I would have had a part in helping to elect the first African American president of the United States — and a man I believed could be a great president. My ninety-year-old mother, who had watched my lifelong fight for civil rights and racial equality, put it this way at a larger family meeting the next day: "So let me get this straight, honey. The first African American in history who has a chance to be president says he needs your help to win — *and you said no.*"

The decision, even with the family's encouragement, was still difficult. I had been in Washington long enough to watch eight different vice presidents, and I knew the history. The office itself has a long and storied career — as a punch line. Benjamin Franklin suggested the vice president be referred to as "His Superfluous Excellency." Richard Nixon was the victim of what might be the only joke Dwight Eisenhower made in his eight years as president. Eisenhower was asked during Nixon's hard-fought campaign against John F. Kennedy if he could delineate for reporters some of the major decisions his vice president had helped to shape. "If you give me a week," Eisenhower replied, "I might think of one."

When Calvin Coolidge took the job, his predecessor, Thomas Riley Marshall, sent a brief note: "Please accept my sincere sympathies." Marshall was a man who brought a towering humility and a bright sparkle of humor to the office. A vice president is a "man in a cataleptic fit," he once said. "He cannot speak; he cannot move; he suffers no pain; he is perfectly conscious of all that goes on, but has no part in it."

Marshall was only a short time in office when he started to explain the job this way: a woman had two sons; one ran away to sea and the other was elected vice president; neither was ever heard of again. Thomas Riley Marshall spent eight years as vice president, helped to steer the country through World War I, then entered history's witness protection program. The identity of Woodrow Wilson's vice president is a question that would have *Jeopardy* fans dialing the complaint lines. But at least Marshall appeared to maintain his good cheer. Nelson Rockefeller was in office for only two years but quickly soured. "I go to funerals," he complained. "I go to earthquakes."

Most vitriolic of all was Daniel Webster, who balked at his party's nomination to be William Henry Harrison's running mate in 1840. "I do not propose to be buried until I am really dead and in my coffin," he would say. Webster miscalculated the upside of the position. Harrison became the first sitting president to die in office — only a month after his inauguration — which would have given Webster a full four-year term as president. Webster turned down the vice presidential nomination again eight years later, then watched Zachary Taylor become the second sitting president to die in office, after only sixteen months.

I wrestled for a day or two with the idea of actually *serving* as anybody's vice president. What worried me most was that I would be doing something I had not done in almost forty years: working for somebody else. As my former chief of staff and longtime friend Ted Kaufman said to me while I was deciding, "I don't want to be in the vice president's office the first day when the president's chief of staff comes in and gives you an assignment." I saw his point. "I never had a boss," I said to Jill once. "I don't know how I'd handle it." Actually, I must have said it to her a good deal more than once. "What happens when I have to support administration policy I don't agree with?" . . . "What's it going to be like to be number two?" . . . "I've never *had* a boss. How am I going to handle this?" Until Jill finally had an answer: "C'mon, Joe," she said. "Grow up."

I agreed to go through the vetting process, but not with a whole lot of enthusiasm.

The team investigating me pored over my finances to make sure I didn't have any major conflicts. They examined my bank accounts, assets, mortgages, bills, and other debts. They wanted to see my tax returns going back ten years, any outside business I may have had, and any stocks. There wasn't much there. I had no business interests; I owned no stocks and bonds. We had the equity in our home and my pension. Jill had a teacher's pension and some certificates of deposit her mother had given her. "This all there is?" Obama asked the team investigating me. The next time I saw him, after the process was concluded, Barack looked at me and joked, "That was one of the easiest vets in the world. You own nothing."

The last of many sessions I had with the vetting team took place in my office, just off the floor of the Senate. There were eight or nine lawyers going through the final details, following up on the few residual questions they had. As the meeting was breaking up the lead attorney said to me, "Well, just one last question, Mr. Chairman, and we're all finished. Why do you want to be vice president?"

"I don't want to be," I said.

"Seriously, Mr. Chairman, why do you want to be vice president?"

"I don't want to be vice president," I repeated. "If he wants me to do it and thinks it will help, I will."

Somehow that conversation got back to my family. They weren't happy, because they thought I might be trying to sabotage my prospects.

I remember exactly when it became clear to me that this would be the right thing to do. Barack had me flown in secret to Minneapolis during a campaign rally. Wearing jeans, a ball cap, and sunglasses, I was sneaked into his hotel suite, where we had the single most significant conversation of our early relationship. I already knew from the presidential primary debates and from working with him on the Foreign Relations Committee that we did not have substantive differences on the issues. What differences there were, were tactical. But I asked him in Minneapolis if he really meant what he said: that he wanted me to help him govern, especially in foreign policy matters. He said he did. And I asked him if he meant what he said about the restoration of the middle class being a defining issue of his presidency.

"Yes," he said. "I really mean it."

I believed him. I was convinced he was an honest and thoroughly honorable man who kept his word. I was also convinced that he could be a really good president.

Barack asked me at that clandestine meeting what specific areas I wanted to take a lead in. My response was I didn't want any specific area. After thirty-five years in the Senate, engaging on almost every major issue, I felt I could offer much more than that. I wanted to have an impact on *all* areas. I would do whatever he most needed me to do, I told him, and promised to be a vocal supporter and defender of his policies. But I wanted more than a set of specific tasks that drew sharp limits on the office. "I want to be the last guy in the room on every major decision," I told him. "You're president. I'm not. I get it. But if it's my experience you're looking for, I want to be the last guy to make the case."

The only remaining question after that was how I'd fit with the incredibly effective team Barack had put together. And it was clear that really mattered to him. So he asked me to meet with his campaign manager and chief strategist to talk about what my role in the campaign would be. They flew into New Castle Airport in secret in a private plane, and Beau and Jill picked them up and drove them to my sister's house so no press would be alerted. It was an important meeting, and when we parted I think we were all convinced that it would work.

I was in a reception room waiting for Jill to get out of the dentist's chair when Barack called with his final decision. He asked me to be his running mate, and I accepted without hesitation. It felt good to say yes.

"I'm looking forward to it," he said.

"So am I."

Half an hour after I accepted, Jill and I walked through our front door and found Ashley sitting in the kitchen. She must have seen something in our faces. "Daddy," she said, "he called, didn't he?"

"Yes, he did."

"And you said yes?"

"I told you I would, honey," I said. "Yes. I accepted."

She jumped up and threw her arms around me. "Daddy, you know how you're always quoting Seamus Heaney's poem," she said. I think everybody in the family could recite *The Cure at Troy* by heart at that point, they'd heard me quote it so many times over the years:

History says, don't hope
On this side of the grave.
But then, once in a lifetime
The longed-for tidal wave
Of justice can rise up,
And hope and history rhyme.

"Dad, this is hope and history."

"Oh, great," I joked. "He's hope. And I'm history."

But I knew what she meant, and I was happy that she was so happy. We got on the phone and told the entire family. And I didn't doubt for one moment that we had made the right decision.

When I was being considered for vice

96

president and reached out to Walter Mondale for advice, he told me his weekly lunch with President Jimmy Carter turned out to be the cornerstone of their working relationship. So Barack and I decided to follow that advice as a way to make sure we had regular meetings where we could talk to each other privately, and with absolute honesty, about anything that was on our minds. We started having our weekly lunch meeting the first month we got to the White House. Even six years in, I still looked forward to them. Not that we didn't spend plenty of time together already. From the outset he included me in all his key meetings. We must have spent a thousand hours together in the Situation Room by then. We started every day in the Oval Office for the daily intelligence briefing. I was at the weekly Principals Committee meeting of his national security team, meetings with foreign policy and economic advisers, his bilateral meetings with visiting heads of state, and meetings with congressional leaders. It didn't take long for me to figure out that it was not just pro forma. The president wanted my read on everything that was happening, and he wanted me around. Almost everybody who comes into contact with a president is hungry for something — sometimes nothing more than an acknowledgment, or simply to be put at ease, but most of all to be *heard*. There was no escaping that for Barack, and it could be draining. "Why do they need so much attention?" he complained to me one day after a congressional delegation left the office. "They constantly have to be reinforced." He knew the answer without my telling him, but he was frustrated by the amount of time and energy it took. And he was happy to have me there to carry some of that load.

One of his longtime personal aides told me once, near the end of our final term, that she had gotten curious and done the math, and it looked to her like the president and I spent about four and a half hours together on the days we were both in Washington. I'm not sure either of us had a chance to spend that many waking hours with our wives on those days. But for all that time together, the president and I were rarely alone, except for fleeting moments between meetings. Our lunches were the one setting where we could talk frankly, without fear of being overheard. We could discuss the most important issues facing the administration, the country, and the world at that moment; and we could talk through any personal issues we were having. If something one of us had done angered or disappointed the other, the weekly lunch was the time to clear the air. Not that there was much of that. Even a "Biden gaffe" that sent the White House and 2012 campaign staff into paroxysms — when I got out ahead of the president by saying on *Meet the Press* that I was "absolutely comfortable" with gay marriage and that gay couples were entitled to all the same civil rights and civil liberties as heterosexual couples — didn't cause any real disturbance between us. I went into the Oval Office the day after and the president just stood up and walked around his desk with a big grin on his face. "Well, Joe," he said, "you told me you weren't going to wear any funny hats or change your brand." He joked that I had sent everybody into an uproar and said the campaign *did* have some work to do, but he didn't take me to task for speaking my mind about an issue I cared about deeply.

The conversation at our lunches was just as often personal. We talked about our wives. We talked about the close friendship between his daughters and my grandchildren, and what was going on in their lives. We talked about golf.

"You know what has surprised me?" the president said to me at one of our earlier lunches. "How we have become such good friends."

"Surprised *you!*" I joked.

As I walked into the Oval Office for our weekly lunch on January 5, 2015, almost six and a half years after I accepted the vice presidency, President Obama was, as usual, at his desk. "C'mon. You hungry?" he said, and led me back past the little study off the main office and into his private dining room. The setting was formal. The president kept only a few personal possessions in the room — some pictures of his daughters and a pair of red boxing gloves, in a glass case, signed by Muhammad Ali. We shed our suit coats and walked to opposite ends of a six-foot-long mahogany table. He complimented me on a job well done at the police memorial in New York.

"What do you have for today?" the president said, as we sat.

Barack was just back from his Christmas vacation in Hawaii and he seemed to have an extra degree of calm in his already placid demeanor. The last midterm election of his political career was behind him, and though it hadn't gone well for us Democrats, the president would never again have to stand and be judged by voters. He still had two years in office, and he was determined to make them count. There were big things out there for us to accomplish, and he had a list of priorities to talk over at lunch that day. The president was one of the few people I had told about Beau's battle with cancer. I felt I had to tell him, because there were times when I had to clandestinely fly to Houston or to Philadelphia for procedures or consultations, and Beau wanted to keep everything private. He did not want this to be a press story, and Barack fully understood. I knew I could count on the president to keep it under wraps. But I also knew that the president still needed me, because all the major initiatives I was responsible for could not be easily handed off to somebody else. I wanted to reassure him that he could count on me, that I wouldn't let anything fall through the cracks.

The power of the presidency had grown enormously during my time in Washington, and the public expectations of what a president can and should accomplish had grown with it. The gravity of the issues he or she faces on a weekly basis is overwhelming; nothing gets to a president's desk that isn't momentous and pressing. And everything but locusts had hit this young president's desk — from his first day on the job.

Barack Obama was sworn into office in the middle of the worst global financial crisis in four generations. The situation was so dire that the entire economic team met in the Oval Office for an hour every day to plan how to deal with the unfolding crisis. "No matter what we do," the president's chief economist told us shortly after we took office, "we're going to continue to lose hundreds of thousands of jobs a month for at least six months." Major banks were failing. The economy was careening off a cliff. Americans were losing their homes, their health care, and their life savings. They were losing hope. Diminishing tax revenues were squeezing federal, state, and local governments. Cities were near bankruptcy, forced to lay off so many teachers and police officers that the American pillars of education and public safety were becoming shaky. President Obama also inherited hot wars in Iraq and Afghanistan, and no clear strategy for victory in either. The wars were costing us nearly fifteen billion dollars a *month* at a time when we could least afford it.

Even Barack Obama, talented and capable as he is, could not possibly have done it all. Like all modern presidents, he was obliged to delegate big pieces of the executive business to his cabinet secretaries, his national security specialists, his chief of staff, and his vice president. But that requires trust. And it was clear from the outset to everyone who knew him that President Obama did not easily place his trust in others. He "travels light," one staffer said of him. Obama's improbable rise in politics — he was a little-known state legislator from the South Side of Chicago in 2003 and president of the United States five years later — was based in part on the fact that he did travel light. Barack Obama did not appear to *belong* to anyone except Michelle and his daughters — not campaign donors, or labor leaders, or civil rights groups, or even friends. I think voters intuited that he would not permit political debts, racial identity, personal attachment, or emotion to cloud his judgment on any big decision. They really believed he would call it as he saw it.

The president had the further benefit of near absolute self-sufficiency; unlike most people I know, his own sense of his worth seemed entirely independent of what other people thought of him. He was almost never ruffled by the slights and unfair criticisms I saw him endure. There were times when I got so irritated at the way people disrespected him — the president, right in the Oval Office — that I was ready to lay into them. Barack knew when I was angry on his behalf and he would occasionally tell me to back off. "Hey, Joe," he would say, "you've got to take the good with the bad." I knew he could defend himself just fine when he was moved to do so, and I usually let it pass, but there were times when I couldn't help myself. "Don't talk about the president that way," I growled at one former Democratic Senate colleague, who said that while she agreed with the president, she didn't like him. "Don't talk about my friend that way," I said. "We're going to have a problem."

Not that I didn't get frustrated with the president on occasion. He never gave me a reason to doubt his strategic judgment in eight years of close-up observation. And there was rarely any daylight between us in matters of policy. But sometimes I thought he was deliberate to a fault. "Just trust your instincts, Mr. President," I would say to him. On major decisions that had to be made fast, I had learned over the years, a president was never going to have more than about 70 percent of the information needed. So once you have checked the experts, statistics, data, and intelligence, you have to be willing to rely on your gut.

There were times when we were unhappy

with each other, but when he was upset with me I heard about it in private, not on the nightly news. At the end of the day I was appreciative that he was straight with me. And the few times I was really upset with him, I was straightforward and direct about my anger. I made no bones about it. But that's how friends treat one another. They level. I think those occasions actually deepened our relationship.

I felt like he treated me as much as an equal as a president is able to. He never gave me an order. "I don't keep Joe's schedule," he would tell staff, "and Joe doesn't keep mine." Most important to me, he honored the one request I had made of him before I accepted his offer to be vice president. Obama reportedly joked with his campaign team that he had said to me, "I want your advice, Joe. I just want it in ten-minute, not sixty-minute, increments." But he kept his end of the bargain, all the way through to the end. He invited me in to be the last person in the room to offer counsel before any big decision was made.

I offered what advice and wisdom I could, but I also tried to offer simple encouragement. The cares of the presidency sit heavy on any person in that office, and there were times when Barack got down. He would become quieter, more reflective, and more withdrawn. He had a distant look. When I saw him start to retreat like that, I always made a point to stick around after our next meeting in the Oval Office. I would wait until everybody else filed out and close the door behind them. "Remember, Mr. President," I would say when it was just the two of us, "the country can never be more hopeful than its president. Don't make *me* 'Hope.' You gotta go out there and be 'Hope.' "

We spent so much time together that we developed unspoken cues and inside humor to ease the pressures of office. Sometimes he would muse out loud: Why would Senator X do this? And why would Congressman Y do that? It was so gratuitous, or so unnecessary, or so impolite. Why? And I would tell him about my uncle Ed Finnegan, who had an answer for this kind of thing that was not exactly specific but always satisfying. "Ya know, Joey," Uncle Ed would say, "there's no accountin' for horses' asses." And Uncle Ed's line became a key bit of shorthand between us, a private joke. When one foreign head of state came to the White House for a visit, he strutted into the Oval Office and almost the first thing out of his mouth was this: "They say I am strong,

Barack, and you are weak. I tell them, 'No, no. You are strong, too.' " We just looked at one another, and the president, cool as always, turned to me, raised an eyebrow and said, "Uncle Ed."

The president did hand me plenty of specific jobs right from the start and didn't look over my shoulder. At a meeting of Obama's foreign policy and national security team a few weeks after we were sworn in, when the president's foreign policy principals said they were prepared to present a plan for keeping the president's campaign commitments on Iraq, the president turned to the group and said, "Joe will do Iraq. He knows it. He knows the players." He made me the sheriff of our first crucial piece of legislation, enacted less than a month after we took office: the American Recovery and Reinvestment Act of 2009. He tasked me with getting the votes we needed in Congress, then left it to me to make sure the $787 billion appropriated in the stimulus package was spent fast and spent well, avoiding the waste and fraud that always accompany big public-works bills. When budget negotiations between the president and the Republican House Speaker — or among congressional leaders — became irreparably broken, the president dispatched me to the Hill to work out a deal with my former colleagues and to make sure we got the votes for passage. When Vladimir Putin began a campaign to destabilize Ukraine, the president assigned me Ukraine. When a crisis erupted after unaccompanied children from the Northern Triangle in Central America began pouring across our border, he turned to me and said, "Joe, you've got to fix this."

At one point soon after, the president asked me to take over the job of repairing our wobbly relations across the entirety of the Americas — the Northern Triangle, Brazil, the Caribbean, everything. "Joe, you can do this," the president joked. "You're good at making new friends. And it's in the same time zone." I didn't point out that most of it was not in the same time zone. I just accepted the new assignment. And he knew I wouldn't drop the ball.

The president never said it to me himself, directly, but in a long talk as we headed to an event in Chicago near the end of the first term, Michelle Obama said to me, "He trusts you, Joe."

The trust went both ways, and it gradually became more than merely professional. I came to feel I could depend on him, too. Barack was the first person outside my family to know about Beau's illness. In 2013, the president and I happened to be doing a political event together in Scranton, Pennsylvania, the town where I was born, the day after I got back from our first harrowing visit to the M. D. Anderson Cancer Center in Houston. The rally drew thousands, which gave the president the opportunity to say things to me he never would have been able to utter in private. "Today is a special day for Joe and me," he told the crowd, "because five years ago today, on August 23, 2008, I announced in Springfield, Illinois, my home state, that Joe Biden was going to be my running mate. And it was the best decision that I ever made, politically, because I love this guy. . . .

"And so I just want all of you to know that I am lucky to have Joe — not just as a running mate, but more importantly, as a friend. And we love his family."

In the sixteen months since that week we got the diagnosis, I had been careful not to reveal the true desperation of Beau's situation to anyone outside the family — not even to the president. Barack had inklings that Beau was struggling, but he never pressed for details. And I didn't bring it up often. But in the middle of 2014, when Beau's aphasia was getting worse, he worried that his illness might eventually affect his cognitive capability. And knowing Beau, Hunt and I became concerned that he might feel honor-bound to resign before his term as attorney general was over. The only income he had at the time was his salary. I told the president about this at one of our private lunches.

"What are you going to do?" he asked.

"Well, he doesn't have much money, but we're okay," I said. "Jill and I can take out a second mortgage on our house in Wilmington if we have to. We'll be fine."

"Don't do that," Barack said, with a force that surprised me. I could see him getting emotional. Then he got up out of his chair and walked around behind me and put his hands on my shoulders. "I'll give you the money. I have it. You can pay me back whenever."

We spent the first part of our lunch on January 5, 2015, running through some of the big initiatives I was quarterbacking at the time: Iraq, Ukraine, and Central America. They had become three of our administration's most pressing foreign policy priorities. The president had recently announced his comprehensive long-term counterterrorism strategy to degrade and eventually destroy ISIL in Iraq, Syria, and throughout the Middle East. I was working with the new prime minister in Iraq to shore up his coalition government and get him the resources he needed to roll back some of ISIL's recent gains in that country; and I was trying to convince the president and the prime minister of Turkey to become more active in the fight against ISIL in Syria. My staff was already preparing my early-February trip to the annual Munich Security Conference, where I needed to press our NATO allies for more support for Ukraine in its struggle against Putin. A few weeks after that I was headed to Guatemala for a two-day summit with the leaders of the Northern Triangle countries. My job there was to persuade them that they had to make the hard political choices that would convince the United States Congress to fund their Alliance for Prosperity.

The discussion meandered, as always, toward more personal topics as the lunch wound down. Barack remained preoccupied with the question of my running for president. He had been subtly weighing in against — for a variety of reasons. For one thing, the president recognized the media's increasing appetite for the drama of politics over real policy. The minute I announced I was running for the nomination, Barack and I both knew, coverage in the West Wing would shift from his agenda to my chances. I also believe he had concluded that Hillary Clinton was almost certain to be the nominee, which was good by him. He thought of her as really smart, really prepared, and backed by the formidable campaign machine the Clintons had spent the past forty years engineering. The president had been Solomon-like when pressed by reporters to choose between Hillary and me. "Both Hillary and Joe would make outstanding presidents and possess the qualities that are needed to be outstanding presidents," he had said. "And they've got different strengths, but both of them would be outstanding." But I knew a number of the president's former staffers, and even a few current ones, were putting a finger on the scale for Clinton.

In January 2015 the president was convinced I could not beat Hillary, and he worried that a long primary fight would split the party and leave the Democratic nominee vulnerable in the general election. More than anything, he did not want to see a Republican in the White House in 2017. I got it, and never took issue with him. This was about Barack's legacy, and a significant portion of that legacy had not yet been cast in stone. I didn't think it possible for a new Republican administration to roll back Barack's landmark health care program, or the Violence Against Women Act, or the gains made by the LGBT community. But we both knew that if a Republican won the presidency, he or she could really unravel Barack's legacy on foreign policy. Neither of us wanted that. I think the president was also concerned that if I ran and lost, it would diminish my own legacy. And finally, I think he wondered about my ability to do my job as vice president *and* run for the nomination while dealing with Beau's battle with brain cancer.

When Barack brought it up at lunch that day, he did it with a soft touch. "If I could appoint anyone to be president for the next eight years, it would be you, Joe," he told me. "We have the same values. Same vision. Same goals. You've earned the right to make a decision based on how you feel about the race."

I told him that after watching him do it for the last six years, I had no desire to live in the White House. "It's the most confining thing in the world," the president said, but he didn't stop to dwell on it. He was almost in a reverie about his own future.

He told me his Christmas vacation had allowed him for the first time to picture what the next twenty-five years could be like. "I think I can do more than I was able to do as president," he said. He said he understood how he wanted to spend the rest of his life. "Joe, have you focused on that? How do you want to spend the rest of your life?"

How do you want to spend the rest of your life? It was a hard question for me to answer that day. I wish I could have said, "Sure, I can ride off into the sunset, too, and be satisfied and content." But it wasn't that simple for me. Part of it was my own pride: if I decided not to run, I had to be able to look in the mirror and know that it was not because I was afraid to lose or afraid of taking on the job. I could not live with walking away like that. And then, too, the question of running for president was all tangled up in Beau, and purpose, and hope. Giving up on the presidential race would be like saying we were giving up on Beau. "We can't give up hope, Joe," Jill would remind me. "We can't give up hope." The mere possibility of a presidential campaign, which Beau wanted, gave us purpose and hope — a way to defy the fates.

How do you want to spend the rest of your life? Barack Obama was my friend, but I found myself unable to fully confide in him. This much I knew, I explained to him: I had two choices. I could have a good ten years with my family, laying the foundation of financial security for them and spending more time with them. Or I could have ten years trying to help change the country and the world for the better. "If the second is within reach," I told him, "I think that's how I should spend the rest of my life."

CHAPTER FIVE: KEEPING BUSY

I knew on Monday that it was going to be a hard week — in all ways. The next day, February 3, 2015, was Beau's forty-sixth birthday, not that he wanted me to make a big deal of it. He expected me to keep doing my job, and doing it well, while he was fighting for his life. Beau's effort, fierce but quiet, was inspiring. He had already exceeded the twelve-to-fourteen-month time line of survival for somebody with glioblastoma multiforme. And the most recent scans showed no clear evidence that the few cancer cells Dr. Sawaya was unable to remove were starting to multiply. The mere fact that Beau was hanging tough, determined to do whatever he had to do to make it, gave the entire family hope. From the very beginning, way back in the late summer of 2013, Beau had opted for the most aggressive course his oncologist could chart. When Dr. Yung recommended that Beau endure triple the amount of the standard chemo drug, called Temodar, while also taking part in the first field trial of an experimental drug treatment designed to boost the effect of Temodar, Beau said, "Let's do it." A few months later, when Dr. Yung suggested adding an unapproved but promising new drug to combat one of the mutations that made his tumor especially virulent, Beau said, "Let's do it." Dr. Yung cautioned that while there was evidence in animal studies that the drug worked, there were no human studies to back it up. There could also be uncomfortable side effects. "If there's a skin rash," Beau said, "I'll just wear long sleeves and a baseball cap. All good."

In April 2014, when Beau began having difficulties with his speech about eight months into his treatment, the doctors could not be sure from the scans whether the difficulties were caused by new tumor growth or the delayed effects of his earlier six-week run of radiation. After receiving special permission from the pharmaceutical company, Dr. Yung asked Beau if he could start him on a well-tested drug that might diminish swelling and seal up leaky blood vessels around the tumor bed. Beau said, "Let's do it." The new drug was given intravenously, and the big needle could be incredibly painful, but Beau never complained. Jill knew, though, and she went with him to the weekly procedure in Philadelphia and made sure he got the nurse who was the gentlest and most expert at inserting the IV.

A few months later, in the summer of 2014, Beau went out and bought an expensive new powerboat so he could take Natalie and Hunter out for long rides and fishing on the Susquehanna River or Chesapeake Bay. Beau loved to be on the water — the spray on his face, a fishing rod in his hand — but he had also been careful with his money over the years. I didn't say anything to him or anyone else, but Jill and I both wondered if Beau was starting to accept the idea that he might not have much time. Why wait for a tomorrow that might not come? But it was so easy to quash that anxiety whenever I saw him. He still looked good. He was still exercising. And we all believed, like he did, that if he could just hang on long enough, science might outrun his disease. There were so many things happening in the field. There might be a breakthrough treatment, we told ourselves, or even a cure.

Beau held his own all through that summer, until August 2014, exactly a year after the diagnosis, when he had a sudden loss of strength and numbness in his right arm and right leg. He didn't complain. He didn't panic. "What's next?" he asked his oncologist. "How do we fight this?" Dr. Yung suggested a more potent drug, with likely side effects including nausea, fatigue, mouth sores, and diminished appetite. The drug would also increase his risk for infection, anemia, and even more serious blood diseases. "Okay, Doc," Beau said, "let's do it." I knew he had to be frustrated by then. He had no real control over what the disease or the treatment was doing to his body; no real control over his blood work; no real control over what his scans looked like every two months; no real control over when and how aggressively his tumor might begin to grow again. What he could control, he did. He kept doing his job as attorney general of Delaware, and doing it well. His office won a forty-five-million-dollar settlement from Bank of America for its misconduct before, during, and after the financial crisis of 2008. This brought the total won from the banks for the state and its citizens to $180 million. He persuaded forty-three other state attorneys general to join him in pushing for federal money to provide support for victims of child pornography. The Child Predator

Task Force that Beau created and oversaw had arrested and convicted more than two hundred child abusers and rescued 129 children from abusive situations by then. "My focus from the beginning has been to protect the most vulnerable among us," he said, "and no one is more vulnerable than our children."

And Beau also kept going home at night to be with Hallie, Natalie, and Hunter. "I read to my children every night," he said to the advanced practice nurse in Houston, Eva Lu Lee, the first time they ever met. "I need time to read to my children." He insisted on climbing to the top of a beautiful mountain trail on our family trip to the Tetons, even though his weak leg made it a real struggle. Beau refused to burden anybody outside of his brother, Hunter, with his actual dread, not even his mother or me.

So tomorrow was his forty-sixth birthday, February 3, 2015, but he did not want to make a big to-do. And besides, Beau reminded Jill, this was Hunter's year. Hunt's birthday is the day after Beau's, and the two of them had always alternated years on who got to pick the birthday meal. "Chicken potpie, right, Mom?" Hunter would say. "Homemade."

■ ■ ■

I had a full schedule that week, as I had almost every week since Beau's diagnosis. I had planned it that way. When I got back to Washington after we learned Beau had brain cancer, I called my chief of staff, Steve Ricchetti, into my office to talk. Steve knew the whole family had been down to M. D. Anderson with Beau and he knew that we had returned with bad news. But he didn't know how bad it was. "I'm just going to tell you this is very serious and it's going to be a very difficult time," I said to Steve as we both settled into our chairs in my West Wing office. "The only way I'm going to get through this is if you just keep me busy. Schedule me. Try to keep everything that we would normally be doing. Keep it in front of me, and keep me working."

Steve is an easygoing guy who had proven willing to do almost anything I asked, but I could tell by the way he was looking at me that this request went against his natural humane instincts. "Look, Steve, this is going to be hard on you, too, but I'm pleading with you to do this for me," I explained. "I know what's best because, unfortunately, I've lived through this before. The only way

121

I survived, the only way I got through it, was by staying busy and keeping my mind, when it can be, focused on my job."

Steve said he would do whatever I asked of him, and he was as good as his word. There were a few times in the next eighteen months when Jill pulled Steve aside to talk. "Joe's working too hard," she would say. "He's exhausted. He's not sleeping. It's going to kill him." It put Steve in a tough spot. He agreed with Jill. There were times when he thought my schedule bordered on cruel, but he was under strict orders from the boss. Steve had also come to believe that part of my insistence on keeping up with the demands of my job was a desire to prove to Beau and Hunt and Ashley that I was fine. That I was still capable of handling anything and everything that was asked of me.

"I would be happy to do anything he'd *let* me do," Steve would say to Jill, diplomatically. And then the two of them would conspire to get me to ease off for a while. I would hear them out when they made the case to me and say no to a few events or meetings — before going right back to the fifteen- or sixteen-hour workdays. Then Jill would call Steve again and say, "This has to stop," and Steve would say he agreed. And sometimes when we were at home alone, Jill would say the same to me — "You've got to stop, Joe. You're going to get run down and you're going to get sick. I'm really worried about you" — only I wasn't so quick to agree.

Steve and Jill worried more than they needed to, was the way I saw it. When I looked at my schedule for the first week in February 2015, I noticed there was a lot to do, some of it truly significant — but all of it was doable.

My daily schedule card for that Monday even looked a little thin — a series of meetings in the White House and lunch with the president. But I was headed overseas in three days, and there was a lot of unfinished business I wanted to push forward before I left town. So Monday was my best chance to focus on the serious work I needed to do with the Congress. First on the list was keeping up our relations with the opposition party. I got hold of the Republicans' new House majority leader to invite him to a breakfast at the Naval Observatory, where the two of us could sit in private and talk about where we might find some ground for cooperation on the budget, or infrastructure spending, or immigration legislation. I had worked hard to develop a relationship with Majority Leader Eric Cantor, but now that Eric had lost his seat, I had to start over with Kevin McCarthy.

I had some follow-up to do for the secretary of energy, Ernest Moniz, who had been asking me to take the lead in pushing a $15 billion initiative to rebuild the country's aging energy infrastructure. This was an urgent and much-needed fix. Power outages caused by storms, especially along the shorelines, were costing Americans billions of dollars a year because the electricity grid needed to be modernized. An inexcusable number of the nation's water pipelines were still made of *wood*. Gas lines around the country were springing leaks, and no wonder. Many had been put in the ground back when Eisenhower was president. Dangerous amounts of methane gas were escaping into the atmosphere at every stage of the natural gas supply chain. My job was to sell the plan to key members of the House and the Senate, and I was hoping to get real bipartisan support. Fixing the gas supply lines, for instance, was not only a necessary safety precaution; it would also improve efficiency in the oil and gas industry and create jobs. So I called Jim Inhofe, a Republican senator from one of the leading oil-producing states, to persuade him that if Congress appropriated money to dig up and replace failing pipe segments and bad connectors, it would be a win for oil and gas producers *and* a win for environmental groups.

Then I placed a call to a congressman from a district just north of New York City to see if he might soften his opposition to the nuclear deal Secretary of State John Kerry was negotiating with Iran. Then I called Senator Tom Carper, from my home state, to touch base with him on the Iran deal and on the Northern Triangle, and to bring him up to date on the effort to get money set aside for the Army Corps of Engineers to deepen the Delaware River channel. After that I added calls to four other legislators who were pushing the Delaware River project.

I even managed to squeeze in a brief phone chat with the president of the University of Delaware, who wanted me to consider setting up some sort of Biden policy center at my alma mater after I left office in two years. And that got me thinking about what I was going to be doing in two years, which once again brought up the question of running for president. I had just bought myself some time by announcing on one of the morning shows that I wouldn't be making a decision until late summer or early fall. And I was expecting a memo on the race from Mike Donilon, my chief political strategist and good friend, any day.

I already knew Mike believed strongly that I should run, and he had been making serious arguments about why I would win. But we had been talking fitfully about 2016 for almost two years now, and I'm sure Mike was getting anxious about the entire enterprise. He never pushed, because he is a kind and considerate man, and he knew Beau wasn't doing well — though I was careful in the way I talked about it. Had I admitted to Mike or anybody else at the time that Beau's illness might make it impossible for me to run, he would have known Beau was in real trouble. And Beau did not want anyone outside the family to know, not even good friends. So I had simply asked both Mike and Steve to do whatever they could to put me in a position to mount a serious campaign, if I did decide to run. Mike approached this charge from me as both a political technician and a friend. He's observant and perceptive, and he'd been by my side for more than twenty years, so he understood without me saying it: keeping alive the possibility of running was important to my spirit. He knew that having that goal visible, even way out on a far and perhaps unreachable horizon, helped get me through the day.

President Obama raised the 2016 race again at our private lunch that day, once we had dispensed with the serious policy talk. He knew I was being pressured by a number of people to get into the race, and he had heard about the Draft Biden movement, complete with bumper stickers — I'M RIDIN' WITH BIDEN. The president was urging caution. He wanted me to make sure I didn't let this chatter get too loud. He didn't want me to look fickle if I decided I was not going to run. "I'm very protective of your legacy," he said. "I really mean it." I assured him I wasn't doing anything to promote the effort; that Mike Donilon was about to hand me a memo about how to run, if I did run, but that I was a long way from the decision. He said I should take my time and really digest Mike's memo. I should approach the decision methodically — plug in all the poll numbers and political variables and seek advice from outside my own team. He suggested I talk to his pollster and his chief strategist and let them read Mike's paper. He said they could be trusted to keep it quiet. "They're the best numbers guys in the country," the president said. "Hillary would have them in a minute if she could." I guess he didn't know that at least one of them was *already* helping Hillary. Then Barack said he would be glad to read the memo, too, and give me his assessment. "I'll be blunt with you," he promised.

Two days later I was having breakfast at the Naval Observatory with Hillary Clinton — a meeting she had requested. She had not yet announced her candidacy or even said if she was going to announce. But she was already assembling a big campaign structure and beginning to poach some of my staff, so her closest advisers had been encouraging her for weeks to reach out to me and make nice. The Clinton campaign hands thought the meeting was worth it, though they were sure that whatever she disclosed to me would leak. I think she knew better.

Hillary arrived at eight o'clock that Wednesday morning and we sat at a dining table in the small library, just behind the main reception room. She and I used to have regular meetings in that room when she was secretary of state and came over for breakfast to get my take on how she was doing with the president. Barack was a tough boss to read, especially for people who didn't spend much time around him, so I think she used me as her Obama whisperer. But Hillary had an entirely new agenda that February morning, and she got right to it. She started off by telling me what a good vice president I had been, how much I had done for the country in my career, and how I had earned the right to run for president. Then she pretty much asked me straight up if I was going to jump in. I didn't feel like I could tell her the truth about Beau. "I'm not in any position to make a decision now" was all I said, "and I think I'm going to wait." If I did enter the race for the Democratic nomination, I assured her, I would be running *for* the nomination, not against her. I would run because I believed I was the best-suited nominee for the moment. But if I ran, I told her, I would not run a negative campaign. She said the same. "Although some of our supporters can get out of hand sometimes," she noted, "it would not be me."

Hillary told me she had thought long and hard about it, and she had decided to seek the nomination. "I have so much respect for you and all that you've done," she said, "and I just wanted to tell you personally." She told me she wasn't ready to announce right away, and she would appreciate it if I kept it quiet. Which I did. I told no one.

As I walked her to the front door on her

way out, I was pretty sure Hillary hadn't gotten all she had come for that morning. I think she had been hoping to hear me say I was standing down. That I wasn't going to seek the nomination. But I couldn't do that yet. I walked her to the door, gave her a warm embrace, and said good-bye.

I felt a little twinge of sadness for Hillary as I watched her walk down the steps that morning. She was as determined as always and confident that she could do the job. She was also running well ahead of me and every other potential Democratic candidate in the very early polls. The sage political analysts would say she was probably on the way to a historic victory — the first woman to win the White House. But she did not evince much joy at the prospect of running. I may have misread her entirely that morning, but she seemed to me like a person propelled by forces not entirely of her own making. And I had absolutely no doubt she understood how brutal the campaign would be for her. What she was about to do took real courage.

It felt like relief to be in the air the next morning, flying east over the Atlantic Ocean, into the rising sun, and headed for serious and consequential business. Added to that, I had my sixteen-year-old grand-daughter, Finnegan Biden, with me for the entire trip. I had made sure the final stop in Europe, right down the road from my last official meeting, would really be just private time for Finnegan and me. The vice presidency had lived up to Jill's hopes of a new adventure for the entire family. One of the great privileges of the office was being able to take my older grandchildren around the world. It was an incredible educational experience for them, and not a burden for me or my staff. At least one of them had been to every continent save Antarctica. I had watched my younger grandchildren, Natalie and Hunter, as they floated in the Dead Sea, met the king of Jordan, and visited the United Arab Emirates and the Persian Gulf. I witnessed my oldest grand-daughter, Naomi, try out her college Mandarin at a state dinner in China; saw her youngest sister, Maisy, meet new friends in Egypt, Kenya, Tanzania, and Sierra Leone, then play pickup soccer on the field where South Africa was hosting the World Cup finals; watched Finnegan assess the North Korean military presence from our perch looking across the DMZ. She thought it would make a great school paper.

"They have all this artillery," she told me

later, pointing at a map, "like big cannons, right, Pop?"

"Yes," I said.

"You realize the North Koreans can take out a *hundred and twenty thousand* people in Seoul, and probably a lot more, if they unleash all of their artillery?" she said, pointing at the map again. "The artillery is up here in this territory."

Finnegan had been the most insistent of all my grandchildren. She called me up one morning in early 2011, about halfway through the first term, just as it hit the newspapers that I was making my first trip to Moscow as vice president. She was twelve. "Pop," Finnegan said, "can I go to Russia with you?"

"Honey, you have school," I reminded her.

"Pop, if you say something to Daddy and tell the teacher, I'll learn a lot more on this trip than I would in school," she explained. "They'll say yes. And remember, Pop. Eastern Europe and Russia is my territory."

Hunter's daughters were a bit like the Great Powers of the late nineteenth century. They had carved out their own spheres of influence around the globe. "Remember, Naomi is China and the Far East," Finnegan said. "Maisy is Africa. *I'm* Europe."

She ended up getting permission to make

the trip, with a little push from me, and was at my side the whole time. We stopped first in Helsinki, where Finnegan got to meet the president and the prime minister of Finland — both of them women. On the plane ride to Moscow afterward somebody on my staff turned to Finnegan and said, "Isn't it amazing meeting two women who run that country?"

"You know what's more amazing?" Finnegan answered. "Almost half the members of the Parliament are women."

There were only a few places Finnegan was not allowed to go with me on that trip. She had to wait patiently in an anteroom at Vladimir Putin's private office in Moscow when I had my meeting with the Russian leader. Putin was biding his time as Russia's prime minister while his protégé, Dmitry Medvedev, sat as a temporary placeholder in the presidency. President Obama had been working hard to strengthen our relationship with the Russian government. Our administration had convinced Medvedev (which really meant Putin) to sign a major new treaty that called for an enormous bilateral reduction of nuclear weapons, but the relationship was already showing new strains. I was in Moscow to make the case that Russia had no reason to fear the recent redeployment of launchers for the missile defense shield in Europe, which was designed to intercept attacks from Iran. Putin was not happy that the launchers were to be repositioned in countries so near his border, like Poland and Romania, and kept asserting that the interceptors were aimed at Russian missiles. He had already sent Medvedev out to make threats about walking away from all the nuclear arms treaties, old and new, which would land the world back in a new cold war. I was there to explain the planned changes to the system, to offer complete transparency in deployment and operation, and to assure Putin that it was not designed to — nor would it — interfere with Russia's own strategic defenses.

I wasn't sure just what I was walking into. President George W. Bush famously said he had looked into Putin's eyes and got "a sense of his soul." I wanted to see for myself. While I had been encouraged by Putin's willingness to sign on to the nuclear arms treaty, I thought the Russian leader had proven himself unworthy of our trust in almost every other instance. Our meeting that day did nothing to dispel that notion. It was long and contentious. Putin was ice-cold calm throughout, but argumentative from start to finish. I explained that as long as Iran was a nuclear threat, it was in our vital interests to protect the United States and our allies in Europe. He changed the subject, complaining that the previous administration had lied to him and had publicly attacked his record on human rights. I pulled out maps to show him the proposed trajectory of the interceptors, to assure him that our missile defense system was not aimed at his ICBMs. He disagreed vehemently and called in his own military advisers to back him up. The meeting went on for hours and ranged through other points of contention. I explained to Putin, for instance, that while we strongly objected to the Russian occupation of parts of Georgia, we were not encouraging Georgian president Mikheil Saakashvili to make trouble. "I speak to Saakashvili regularly on the phone and I urge him not to take provocative actions, just as I urge you to restore Georgia's sovereignty," I said. "Oh," Putin replied, "we know exactly what you say to Mr. Saakashvili on the phone."

We never got near a satisfactory mutual agreement about the missile shield. We would keep him informed, I finally told Putin, but we were going ahead with the planned redeployment. He was not happy.

As the meeting was coming to an end, Putin asked me to have a look around his office. The furnishings were elaborate and impressive. "It's amazing what capitalism will do, isn't it?" I said, gazing up at the high ceiling. "Magnificent."

As I looked back down, I was face-to-face with him.

"Mr. Prime Minister, I'm looking into your eyes," I told him, smiling. "I don't think you have a soul."

He looked at me for a second and smiled back. "We understand each other," he said.

And we did.

Out over the Atlantic that Thursday afternoon, four years later, cruising at more than six hundred miles an hour, I sat in my small private cabin reading through the briefing books and talking with my trusted foreign policy staff about what exactly we needed to accomplish on the trip. Air Force Two would be touching down that evening in Brussels, where I had meetings scheduled with the highest-ranking leaders of the European Union and a one-on-one with the prime minister of Belgium the next day. But that was just warm-up for the critical business at the Munich Security Conference that weekend. The security conference was like coming full circle and facing a new reckoning with Vladimir Putin, who was once again president of the Russian Federation — and acting badly. I had been to the Munich Security Conference in 2009, just three weeks after we took office, to make a speech laying out President Obama's major goals in foreign policy to a world audience. Part of that speech was meant for Putin.

The Russian leader needed to hear the president's commitment to European security, as well as his desire to have Russia as a partner in that effort. Our new administration supported "the further strengthening of European defense, an increased role for the European Union in preserving peace and security, a fundamentally stronger NATO-EU partnership, and a deeper cooperation with countries outside the Alliance who share our common goals and principles," I said. "The United States rejects the notion that NATO's gain is Russia's loss, or that Russia's strength is NATO's weakness. . . .

"It is time — to paraphrase President Obama — it's time to press the reset button and revisit the many areas where we can and should be working together with Russia. . . . The United States and Russia can disagree and still work together where our

137

interests coincide. And they coincide in many places." I made the president's position crystal clear. We were open to cooperation, but there were basic ground rules.

"We will not recognize any nation having a sphere of influence," I assured the conference, and everybody in that room understood I meant that the United States and its NATO allies would not permit Russia to force former Soviet republics back into its orbit against their will. "It will remain our view that sovereign states have the right to make their own decisions and choose their own alliances."

Our administration was seeking to promote and extend the liberal international order that had been in place for forty years: a Europe free, whole, and at peace, with each and every independent country having agreed-upon and *secure* borders.

By February 2015, as I headed toward Munich, Vladimir Putin had signaled that he was no longer happy playing by the rules Soviet leaders had accepted as part of the historic and far-reaching Helsinki Accords in 1975. He was willing to test European resolve on the principle of the sanctity of borders, and he was doing so with impunity in Ukraine. My main objective in Munich was to continue to encourage our European allies to stand with us, to make sure Putin understood that Russia would pay a price for bullying a weaker neighbor.

The Ukrainian people had been on a thrilling and sometimes harrowing roller coaster for the previous year, and I felt like I had been on it with them. A popular demonstration, which started at a square in Kyiv in late 2013, when President Viktor Yanukovych reneged on his promise to take the country into the European Union, had grown from a spontaneous eruption to a real political movement — one President Yanukovych mishandled badly. I had known and worked with Yanukovych since 2009, and I knew he was in a tough spot. While popular pressure mounted on Yanukovych to honor his EU pledge, Putin was obviously tightening the screws on him to resist the movement and tie the country more closely to Russia. Yanukovych did not handle the situation well. He resisted the democratic Revolution of Dignity in Maidan Nezalezhnosti with increasing force, eventually loosing his riot police on the streets of Kyiv to disrupt, injure, and finally murder demonstrators. The protesters in the Maidan found themselves in a war zone, enduring a brutal three-month siege in the dead of winter. They refused to back down, even in the face of death, and transformed the square where the protest began into an armed camp. Demonstrators seized administration buildings and erected barricades so they could set up command centers, mess halls, and aid stations for people beaten and bloodied by Yanukovych's uniformed police and his secret plainclothes thugs. The crowds of protesters grew to more than fifty thousand and just kept growing. By the middle of February 2014, they were inching toward the Parliament building.

I made the last of many urgent calls to Yanukovych in late February of 2014, when his snipers were assassinating Ukrainian citizens by the dozens and we had credible reports that he was contemplating an even more vicious crackdown. I had been warning him for months to exercise restraint in dealing with his citizens, but on this night, three months into the demonstrations, I was telling him it was over; time for him to call off his gunmen and walk away. His only real supporters were his political patrons and his operators in the Kremlin, I reminded him, and he shouldn't expect his Russian friends to rescue him from this disaster. Yanukovych had lost the confidence of the

Ukrainian people, I said, and he was going to be judged harshly by history if he kept killing them. The disgraced president fled Ukraine the next day — owing to the courage and determination of the demonstrators — and control of the government ended up temporarily in the hands of a young patriot named Arseniy Yatsenyuk.

Elation in Ukraine was followed by bad news a few days later. Vladimir Putin, displeased that he had lost his puppet in Kyiv, immediately sent a force across the border and annexed the Ukrainian oblast (province) of Crimea. The West condemned the annexation but did little else. And Putin just kept going. He menaced other oblasts in the east of Ukraine for the next six months and sent Russian tank units across the border to slaughter Ukrainians who resisted. A cease-fire he signed in September 2014, the Minsk agreement, did little to hold him back. Nearly a thousand people were killed in the two months after the cease-fire went into effect. The number of internally displaced Ukrainians was climbing toward five hundred thousand, as was the number of Ukrainian refugees. At the beginning of February 2015, as I headed back to Europe, Putin-backed separatists were making an assault on Ukrainian soldiers holding Debaltseve, a strategic road and railway junction fifty miles in from the Russian border. And Putin was doing everything he could to destabilize the Ukrainian economy and force a collapse of the newly elected government in Kyiv.

I was the point man for our administration on the crisis, which was exactly where I wanted to be. There were academics in the news saying Ukraine was bound to be a defeat for the West, and it would be an unwelcome albatross on my neck if I ran for president in 2016. "He's tied to Ukraine policy," a presidential scholar from Pennsylvania told a reporter. "So he could be vulnerable." I didn't much care. There was an important principle at stake: big countries ought not to beat up smaller ones, especially after they had given their word not to. What made the attack on Ukraine particularly galling was that Putin had violated a long-held international norm, as well as an explicit agreement. Ukraine had given up its nuclear weapons program years earlier — in return for a guarantee from the United States, the United Kingdom, *and* Russia to respect its borders and its sovereignty. Two of the three larger countries had kept that promise.

■ ■ ■

We touched down in fog-shrouded Munich
on Friday night, February 6, 2015, and
while Finnegan and I rode in the motorcade
toward the Westin Grand hotel on the dark,
amber-lit, snow-dusted streets, I reflected
on what had to be done in my brief visit to
the city. I had been threading the very narrow eye of a needle for the past year in the
Ukraine crisis. President Obama's sympathies were all with Ukraine, but he was not
going to allow this regional conflict to
escalate into a hot war with Russia. Barack
was a student of modern world history, and
an incisive one. He was always on guard
against the age-old mistake of allowing
smaller brush fires to be unwittingly fed
until they had become terrifying conflagra-
tions beyond anyone's control. And he was
keenly aware that the biggest unforced er-
rors the United States had made after World
War II were not a result of too much restraint, but too little. He would caution me
sometimes about overpromising to the new
Ukrainian government. "We're not going to
send in the Eighty-second Airborne, Joe.
They have to understand that." The president and I agreed that we could and should

convince our European allies to support and extend serious economic sanctions against Russia. But economic sanctions were as far as the United States and its allies in Europe would go.

President Obama was always mindful of the concerns of the Big Four in Europe — Britain, Germany, France, and Italy — whose leaders he was in touch with constantly. The senior member of the quartet, Chancellor Angela Merkel of Germany, was on record with her worry about "a confrontation [in Ukraine] which risks spiraling out of control." She and the others were even more worried about the political backlash they would face at home when the economic sanctions and embargoes on Russia started to pinch their own business communities. And none of them were hot to spend their political capital to save an emerging democracy whose leaders had exhibited a penchant for corruption, self-dealing, and self-destructive behavior. I was probably swayed in my own thinking by my frequent contacts with the leaders of our more recent allies in Europe — in Poland, Romania, the Baltic states, the Balkans. Putin's move in Ukraine felt like the canary in the coal mine to them. They were afraid that if the West didn't stand firm there, Putin might start carving off pieces of their territory near the Russian border. Or more.

It was almost ten at night when Finnegan and the staff and I finally settled into our rooms at the Westin, but I wasn't ready to sleep. I looked over the briefing materials again and started gaming out the next few days. I was going to be giving a speech at the Munich conference Saturday afternoon and had more than half a dozen formal meetings scheduled that weekend. The most important was a trilateral talk just before noon on Saturday with Ukrainian president Petro Poroshenko and Chancellor Merkel. Merkel and French president François Hollande were in the middle of a tense negotiation with Putin about defining and implementing a new and improved version of the shaky Minsk cease-fire. Merkel had a phone call with Putin scheduled for the next day, so I wanted to be there at Poroshenko's side in our three-way meeting to make sure Merkel understood that the United States remained ready to stand tough for him and his nation's borders. But before any of that, I wanted to make sure to be in the audience for Merkel's own address to the security conference. So that was the first thing up on my public calendar — less than ten hours away.

The chancellor was strong in her speech that next morning. Ukraine was "seeing both its territorial integrity and sovereignty disregarded," she said. "International law is being violated." But she was not strong enough for my taste; the passive voice weakened her statement. And I was disappointed when, after her speech, she flatly refused to consider providing any real weaponry to Ukraine's overmatched military. "The progress that Ukraine needs cannot be achieved by more weapons," she said. She seemed to have the sympathy of the crowd on that point.

I left the Merkel event and told my staff we had to revise my own remarks. My words needed to be as direct and declarative as possible. We had less than four hours to fix the speech, and I had to do the meeting with Merkel and Poroshenko first. I instructed my team to start un-lawyering the language of the speech. I wanted them to make absolutely sure that the plain meaning could not be missed, and told them I would be back to help with rewrites as soon as I could.

The room for the meeting with President Poroshenko and Chancellor Merkel was nothing fancy. We sat at a relatively small table in the corner of a conference room,

which meant it was an intimate talk. Poroshenko seemed relieved I was there. He
knew I was committed to Ukraine's success
for its own sake and also as a proof to Russia of European resolve. I thought the
outcome of the Ukraine crisis would set the
tone for central and eastern Europe for
decades, for good or for ill. I had been hard
on Poroshenko since his election nine
months earlier. I'd made it clear to him that
he could not afford to give the Europeans
any excuse for walking away from the sanctions regime against Russia. He had to
continue to fight the elements of corruption
that were embedded in the political culture
of Ukraine's Soviet and post-Soviet governance — both in Yatsenyuk's rival party *and*
in Poroshenko's own. But the Ukrainian
president also knew I had gone to bat for
him to get aid packages from the International Monetary Fund and loan guarantees
from the United States. That I had been
pushing hard at the Principals Committee
meetings to provide training for his military,
and had already been able to get him
nonlethal equipment like the special radars
Ukraine's military needed to identify the
location of Russian mortars. Poroshenko
could not have missed my own sense of
urgency where the future of Ukraine was

concerned.

Poroshenko knew he was in a much stronger position with Merkel as well. Her relationship with Putin had soured over his actions in Ukraine in recent months. Putin was the bad actor here, the chancellor assured Poroshenko at our meeting that day, but she nonetheless pressed him, as she had us, to construct some sort of "off-ramp" for Putin. She was looking for concessions from the Ukrainian president she could take to Putin the next day. She believed the Russian leader needed to be able to walk away and claim some victory. She wasn't specific, but she kept asking Poroshenko to find something he could put on the negotiating table. The term she used for what Putin needed was a "face-saving" way out.

"We can't blame the victim here," I said, nodding at Poroshenko. I pointed out that Putin had not fulfilled any of his commitments under the original Minsk agreement, and *Putin* had to be held accountable for that failure. The Ukrainian leader could offer to give more local autonomy to the different regions, or let Russian be a coequal official language in the easternmost oblasts, or withdraw his heavy artillery from the front lines, but what should come *first* was action from Putin. What should come first was Putin withdrawing his tanks and his soldiers and Putin handing control of the border back to Ukraine. The restoration of Ukraine's border had to come before President Poroshenko conceded anything. Merkel seemed frustrated with me by the time the meeting broke up.

I found myself with very little time remaining to rewrite my speech — a single hour while I ate lunch and another spare half hour after that. I was scheduled to take the podium at three o'clock that afternoon, and at five after three I was still dictating re-worked passages to my speechwriter. *Russia sought to keep secret its little green men and the multiple tanks that they've given the separatists. But we have given you all incontrovertible proof that they exist. You've seen the pictures.* The staff's collective blood pressure was already rising into the red zone by ten after three, when I was still dictating phrases. But I had to get it right. *It is not the objective of the United States of America to collapse or weaken the Russian economy. That is not our objective. But President Putin has to make a simple, stark choice: get out of Ukraine or face continued isolation and growing economic costs at home.* What was fifteen minutes in the grand scheme? What was twenty minutes? Twenty-five?

"Ladies and gentlemen, as the chairman said earlier today, I did stand here six years ago and in the first major foreign policy address of our administration, I spoke about the 'reset,' " I began, thirty-two minutes behind schedule. The speech only ran twenty-eight minutes. I was declarative and I was direct. "America and Europe are being tested," I said. "President Putin has to understand that, as he has changed, so has our focus. We have moved from resetting this important relationship to reasserting the fundamental bedrock principles on which European freedom and stability rest. And I'll say it again: inviolate borders, no spheres of influence, the sovereign right to choose your own alliances. I cannot repeat that often enough. . . . We need to remain resolute and united in our support of Ukraine, as the chancellor said this morning. What happens there will resonate well beyond Ukraine. It matters to all — not just in Europe, but around the world — all who may be subject to aggression."

I came as close as I could to telling our NATO allies that it was our moral duty to provide weapons to Ukraine. The Ukrainians had shown real courage, and though they were unlikely to stop any determined Russian military aggression, I believed they

deserved to be able to try to defend themselves. "Too many times President Putin has
promised peace, and delivered tanks, troops,
and weapons. So we will continue to provide
Ukraine with security assistance, not to
encourage war but to allow Ukraine to
defend itself. Let me be clear: we do not
believe there is a military solution in
Ukraine. But let me be equally clear: we do
not believe Russia has the right to do what
they're doing. We believe we should attempt
an honorable peace. But we also believe the
Ukrainian people have a right to defend
themselves."

I paused for a brief moment, and let the
applause register on every policy maker in
the room. I was hoping the applause would
equal resolve.

When the speech was over, I felt like I had
accomplished what I had set out to, especially after John McCain, who was leading
the United States congressional delegation
at Munich, told me he thought it was the
best speech he had ever heard me give. His
support mattered to me personally, and it
mattered institutionally. Congress controlled
the purse strings. If we needed to get
weapons to Ukraine, Congress would have
to appropriate the money to do so. And
there seemed to be growing bipartisan sup-

port. Even Senator Ted Cruz, who rarely agreed with anything I had to say, agreed with me about providing support to beleaguered Ukrainian fighters. As did Republican senator Lindsey Graham. Chancellor Merkel "can't see how arming people who are willing to fight and die for their freedom makes things better," Lindsey Graham told reporters in Munich. "I do."

It had snowed in Munich early Sunday morning, and the temperature never rose above the freezing mark, so the ground crunched under our feet as my granddaughter Finnegan and I approached the entrance gate near a looming guard tower that afternoon. There was a ninety-five-year-old man at the gate, sitting in his wheelchair, waiting to greet us. I had spent the early part of that day reassuring leaders of a few of our allies in eastern Europe, advising the president of Montenegro on how he might improve his country's chances for an invitation to join NATO, and trying to convince the leader of the Kurdish Regional Government in Iraq to help the new Iraqi president, Haider al-Abadi, in his effort to push ISIL out of their country. Abadi was in Munich looking for help from all quarters, and I spent a full hour with him to offer some much-needed encouragement. He was a little down, and for good reason. When the conference switched topics from Ukraine to ISIL at the end of the first day, one reporter noted, "room clears. No crowd for al-Abadi. Not a good sign." I promised him I was still there for him and would continue to be.

By that Sunday afternoon my official duties for the week were finally behind me, but not my duty as Pop. And I did not take my job as grandfather any less seriously than I did my job as vice president. The last stop in Germany was a guided tour for Finnegan and me of the World War II–era concentration camp at Dachau, a field trip that had become another Biden family tradition. This was a place I felt all my children and grandchildren needed to experience. I had taken Beau and Hunter and Ashley on separate trips to Dachau when they were teenagers, and Finnegan was now of age, too.

My insistence on taking my children and grandchildren to see Dachau had to do with my own father, who used to talk about the horrors of the Holocaust at the dinner table when I was a kid. The discussions were never long, and he didn't preach at us or make any big speeches about Hitler's attempt to exterminate the Jews in Germany, but he imparted real wisdom. Dad would remind us that a campaign of that size could not have been waged in secret. The idea that the German people did not know this was happening defied logic. Humans were capable of incredible cruelty, our father wanted me, my sister, and my brothers to understand. And just as dangerous, he made us see, human beings were also capable of looking the other way and remaining silent when awful things were happening all around them.

The man in the wheelchair, Max Mannheimer, had been a prisoner at Dachau and other concentration camps when he was a young man. He and one brother had survived, but his wife, his parents, his sisters, and another brother had all been murdered. I wanted Finnegan to hear his personal story. I had also given her some reading material in preparation for the trip. Dachau was the first concentration camp put into operation by the Nazis, in 1933. The first prisoners there were Hitler's political opponents — German communists, social democrats, and trade unionists. Then came Jehovah's Witnesses, Roma (Gypsies), homosexuals, and other people the Nazis deemed "undesirable." In the late 1930s the Nazis began to fill the camp with Jews.

Almost thirty thousand prisoners were worked to death or murdered at Dachau between 1940 and 1945. Nobody can say for sure how many were killed at Dachau in the years before that. I assigned Finnegan an essay that included the following poem by Martin Niemöller, a Protestant pastor who was thrown into a German concentration camp at the end of the war.

First they came for the Socialists, and I did
    not speak out —
Because I was not a Socialist.
Then they came for the Trade Unionists,
    and I did not speak out —
Because I was not a Trade Unionist.
Then they came for the Jews, and I did not
    speak out —
Because I was not a Jew.
Then they came for me — and there was
    no one left to speak for me.

Finnegan and I were escorted through the camp by a tour guide and Mr. Mannheimer. It was the same path I had taken with Finnegan's father, Hunter, thirty years earlier, but it was different. It seemed as though things had been rearranged to make visitors less uncomfortable. They had softened the cruel edges over the years, as I should have

155

expected from a line in the Dachau site literature. "As every season has its own charm in Germany," it read, "you can also plan to visit the camp according to your own preference." The bunks in the living quarters at Dachau were still there, so you could see how the Nazis packed tens of thousands of people into the camp. I remembered seeing names carved into the wooden frames of the bunks on earlier visits, but now the bunks appeared clean and varnished.

At first the guide seemed reluctant to take Finnegan and me to the camp's notorious gas chamber, but I insisted. I was thinking of the first time I went there, with Beau, how we walked into that building and they explained to us that the prison guards would tell their victims that they were going to the showers and instruct them to remove their shoes, their clothes, and their false teeth. Then the guides led us into the chamber itself and slammed the door behind us with a frightening clank. There are guides at Dachau today who insist the prisoners were never gassed there, or that it was used only a handful of times. But I wanted Finnegan to see all of that, and I wanted her to see the ovens where the guards cremated the victims after they were shot, hanged, starved to death, killed as part of medical experiments, or actually gassed. Max Mannheimer was a living witness. He had been forced to load into wagons the corpses of victims who had died at nearby work camps, then haul them to the ovens at Dachau to be cremated.

Finnegan saw and heard it all, and then we walked back outside and looked through the fencing at the rows of tile-roofed, middle-class houses just blocks away. The people who lived in those houses in the 1930s and '40s had to have known what was happening inside this prison camp, I wanted her to understand. They were near enough to literally smell the burning human flesh. How could they not know?

The thing I wanted Finnegan to feel was the same visceral jolt that had animated so much of my own career in public life. "Look, honey," I said to Finnegan as we walked back through the gate and back into our own time. "This can happen again. This is happening in other parts of the world now. And you have to speak out. You can't remain silent. Silence is complicity."

CHAPTER SIX:
IT HAS TO BE YOU

The night sky seemed unusually dark and increasingly ominous. The five of us in the library of my quiet home peered out through the big windows and watched as the cloud cover seemed to thicken and push down toward earth. The barometric pressure was rising steeply. The temperature had already fallen below fifteen degrees and was heading toward single digits. We could trace the flight of an occasional snowflake as it fell through the halo of the Naval Observatory's outside lights. But the mood in the room that Thursday night, February 19, 2015, was determinedly upbeat. Mike Donilon and Steve Ricchetti had joined Beau, Hunter, and me to talk through Mike's new twenty-two-page memo about 2016. He had handed it to us nine days earlier, so we had all had a chance to absorb it in detail. Mike's message could not be missed: the presidential race was coming to me.

Mike's memo had laid out the arguments in straight, unornamented prose. The economy was on the rise in early 2015, the memo noted, finally starting to shake free from the last effects of the long, gray recession that had followed the implosion of the financial system. He argued that I had earned the right to claim some credit. From the Recovery Act stimulus, to the stabilization of the banks, to the auto industry rescue, to the numerous knotty budget and tax deals I had negotiated with the Republicans in Congress, I had been a critical partner in shaping and executing the plan that helped President Obama take the country from crisis to recovery to the beginnings of resurgence. Who better than me, Mike argued, to finish the job?

Mike was convinced that the restoration of the badly beat-up American middle class, meanwhile, would be central to the 2016 campaign. Even Republicans were talking about it. And Mike's analysis showed that there was nobody in the field in either party who was more closely identified with the middle class than I was. Middle-class concerns had been central to my entire forty-five-year career in public office, as Mike pointed out. He believed nobody spoke with more understanding and empathy about what the middle class had suffered in recent years, or with more authority about the necessity to remake the bargain the country had long had with decent, hardworking families, or with more credibility about the many opportunities we had to do that.

The voting public was tired of careful and carefully packaged candidates. My reputation as a "gaffe machine" was no longer looking like a weakness. The public could see that I spoke from the heart and I meant what I said. "Authenticity matters," Mike had written. And if the voters craved authenticity, I was at the top of the chart.

I had a long and wide-ranging career in foreign policy, and had met with virtually every world leader. Mike argued that voters believed I knew the challenges the country would face in the near future and had a real strategy for where and how to use our incredible power to greatest effect.

Then, too, my longtime (and legendary in some donor quarters) discomfort at raising huge sums of money to run a campaign — even while going out and raising huge sums of money for the 2008 and 2012 campaigns — might finally be seen as a strength. Voters were increasingly uneasy at the way the Supreme Court's Citizens United decision had permitted, and even encouraged, unlimited campaign spending by a handful of billionaires who seemed to be getting their way on policy matters. "This shouldn't be a holier-than-thou, you're-pure kind of position," Mike wrote, "but one held by someone who knows what's wrong with the system, who's been a part of it, and who can see it spiraling out of control. . . . One of your very first bills (if not the first) as a young senator was to support public financing, and you have a long history on this issue."

The five of us — my two sons, my two closest staff members, and me — spent a few hours going through Mike's main points, and also his last section, about how to proceed from here. His memo laid out a very specific agenda for the next two months: I had just given a speech the previous week in Iowa about my plan to extend the economic recovery to all Americans, and Mike thought I should build on that with a speech in New Hampshire about middle-class dreams; then a speech in Washington laying out the aims of foreign policy in a Biden presidency; then a speech in New York challenging Wall Street and business leaders to look beyond quarterly results and personal bonuses and start meeting their responsibilities to their workers. We also

161

needed to start identifying and hiring key staff and we needed to start building a campaign structure in the early primary and caucus states. Mike thought I should not wait for the summer or fall, but announce my candidacy that April. All of that seemed plausible, except maybe the announcement part. But I also wanted to be sure we didn't schedule anything that intruded on the preparations for my trip to the Northern Triangle the last weekend of February and into March. There was a lot riding on that trip, and I had to be ready.

My eye was drawn to Beau as we talked. His term as attorney general had ended six weeks earlier, so he was no longer pressed by job concerns, and it wasn't yet late in the evening, but he was already tiring. He was so gaunt, and his face seemed drained of color. I could see the outlines of the leg brace through his pants. For more than twenty years, at any meeting about any political campaign, I had looked to Beau for counsel. He was the only other person in the room that night who had ever stood for and won elective office. Beau's advice was the advice I would have most valued at that moment. But that night he mainly just sat and observed. Beau had been losing recall of more and more proper nouns lately, and he seemed less willing to fight through it. Ashley had told me that Beau was no longer inviting her into the room for his speech therapy, because his decline really bothered him. Beau said almost nothing that chilly February night in Washington. He would whisper something to his brother instead, and Hunter would speak for him.

It occurred to me as I watched Beau and Hunter that everybody in that room was playacting to some degree. Whether or not we really bought into Mike's arguments was a secondary consideration that night. It was as if we were all keeping up an elaborate and needful charade. Steve and Mike knew it as well as my sons and I did. We all understood how much Beau wanted me to run for president. We all knew that, more than anything, Beau did not want to be the reason I did *not* run. He would be there for me. He could handle it. Beau was trying to reassure us, and we were trying to reassure Beau. So what were the five of us to do that night but put everything else out of our minds and talk about next steps? I had two speeches scheduled in New Hampshire in six days. We should make sure the focus was on middle-class dreams.

The snow was coming down by the time the meeting began to break up. Hunter lagged behind when everybody else got up to call it a night. "Could we talk, Dad?" he said.

"Sure, honey."

So after Mike and Steve went out to their cars and Beau left with the Secret Service detail that was going to drive him home, Hunt and I went upstairs to our private family space on the second floor. I could see how badly he needed to talk. His older brother's rapid deterioration was really tearing at him. The two of them were headed down to M. D. Anderson in Houston the next week for Beau's regular scans, and as the date approached they were both growing more apprehensive about what the new images would reveal. Hunter was showing the strain. Beau still appeared so calm and so free of emotion to anybody who watched him. *All good. All good.* He was like the proverbial duck on the pond — gliding effortlessly above the surface of the water and paddling like hell below. Only it was Hunter who was his brother's unseen and hard-pressed propeller. I had watched my two sons together — and they were always together. From the time in the hospital after the accident when they were just little boys, to when Hunt helped with the strategy for Beau's first race for attorney general. Forty-five years now. I knew the dynamic. The more Beau battled to keep his emotions in check, the more Hunt would take them on as his own. It was as if Beau wore his emotions on Hunter's sleeve.

"I can't stand Beau being afraid like I know he is, Dad," Hunter said, when we were finally alone.

"That's what bothers me most, honey," I told him. "It's the thing that keeps me awake at night."

A night like tonight, planning out 2016, was a godsend, Hunter said. He was convinced the entire family needed to have this purpose, this outlet. Then Hunter told me that what worried Beau most was that if the worst happened, we would both give up. He said we couldn't let that happen. Hunter told me that at the end of 2012, just after Barack and I were reelected, he and Beau had talked about the future. They thought Beau would win his race for governor in 2016; and then, whether or not I ever made it to the White House, Beau would have his chance to run for president.

"But now," Hunter said, and I knew he was talking for both of them, "it has to be you, Dad."

I had my second call in three days with

President Poroshenko the next morning. He was feeling forsaken. Merkel and Hollande had made the new cease-fire deal with Putin — Minsk II — after Poroshenko acceded to Putin's need for "face-saving." Poroshenko had grudgingly agreed to let Russia control parts of the Ukrainian border until new elections in a few oblasts had been held. And what had it bought Poroshenko? Minsk II looked at the start to be about as useful as Minsk I. Ukrainian separatists with Russian backing had killed at least twenty-eight civilians and Ukrainian soldiers in the hours before the cease-fire was to take effect, and increased its assault on the transportation hub of Debaltseve in the days after. The Russians did not appear to be pulling back much heavy artillery, and there were reports that they had rolled another sixty tanks up to the Ukrainian border. There wasn't a lot more I could do beyond sympathize and tell him we were still with him. I had publicly condemned Putin's blatant new cease-fire violations, and I told Poroshenko I would try to get real monitors to keep score on the agreed-upon withdrawal of Russian tanks and heavy artillery. I reminded President Poroshenko that, fair or not, he still could not give his European allies any excuses to walk away. His own military had to remain pure as Caesar's wife along the border, I told him. They could not do anything that allowed Putin to claim Russian-backed separatists had been provoked. And he and Prime Minister Yatsenyuk had to continue to work together to pass anticorruption and reform legislation if they wanted the International Monetary Fund to keep writing them much-needed checks. I also let him know I would do what I could to help him meet his critical military needs — like antitank weapons. I said the same to Yatsenyuk that morning, but in a separate call. The two men still would not be in the same room together.

I got off the call, gathered my national security staff, and we started to game out how to get additional economic sanctions on Putin and his agents in Ukraine, and how to get the Ukrainian military more equipment and better training. If the Ukrainians were able to make Russia pay a real price for the incursion — like Russian soldiers coming home in body bags — Putin might rethink the wisdom of continuing his attacks.

The day I flew to New Hampshire, Wednesday, February 25, to sing the song of the Obama-led economic recovery and how we

167

needed to do more to extend it into the middle class, was a rough one. I woke up with a scratch in my throat, and by the time I started the first speech of the day at the University of New Hampshire's Rudman Center I was having a hard time suppressing a cough. I was feeling worse by the minute, but I was determined to lay down a marker. "When our government doesn't work, it's not the politicians who get hurt, it's the American people. It's hardworking ordinary Americans who get up every day, go to work, pay their taxes, pay their bills, take care of their families," I said, then I coughed aloud. "Excuse me, I have a cold — and take care of their communities, they're the ones who get hurt — the middle class. And let me tell you something: the middle class has enough to overcome without having to overcome dysfunctional politicians and dysfunctional government." This message mattered. It was important. The defining issue of 2016 was the very real challenges faced by the American middle class: "All we have to do is give the middle class a fighting chance. It's not hyperbole. When the middle class does well, everybody does well. The economy expands, and working-class and poor folks have a way up. Never, ever, ever in the history of the journey of America, when ordinary people have been given a fighting chance, have they ever let their country down. Never. Never. Never. Never."

I did two talks on the theme that day, with long question-and-answer sessions, and I was sure I was connecting with the people in those rooms. They wanted someone to speak to the dreams of the middle class. Someone who understood how tough things had been. Someone who gave them hope that their dreams weren't dead. This was a message people were ready to hear, and one I was sure I could deliver.

By the time I boarded Air Force Two for the return trip to Washington, where I had a meeting to prep for my trip to Central America, I was feeling drained. I had a fever by then and could hear a crackle in my left lung every time I took a deep breath. I went into my private cabin and lay down on the couch. Doc O'Connor came in before takeoff, had a good long look at me, and put me on Mucinex and antibiotics.

I dragged myself out of bed the next morning and went to the office, but as the day wore on, I felt worse. This was not getting better, even with antibiotics. Doc O'Connor came in to check on me and looked worried. This was only the second time I had been sick in the six years he had treated me. My cough was dry but insistent, and my fever was increasing — probably because I had developed pneumonia in my left lung. Doc put me on triple antibiotics and an IV drip to get some fluids back in my system. He came by the residence the next day and pronounced me only marginally improved, if improved at all. Doc told me I was sick enough that I should scrub the upcoming trip to Central America. I was scheduled to fly to Uruguay the next day, Saturday, February 28, spend two days in Uruguay for the new president's inauguration, then two days in Guatemala City for major negotiations with the presidents of the Northern Triangle countries. I told Doc to forget the idea of my staying put. This was too important. I could get some sleep and recover on the plane, and he could stay right by my side to monitor me. But I had to make this trip.

"Sir, I understand pulling down an international trip is a big deal," Doc said. "I get it. It's not good press. It's embarrassing. But you know what else is embarrassing and not good press? Collapsing on camera. You remember the state dinner in Japan when George Bush threw up on the table, right?

If that's the YouTube video you want, go ahead."

"This trip is important, Doc."

"I know this is important, sir, but you have pneumonia. And right now, you look like shit. I can't make you not look like shit." He just kept talking, and I didn't have the strength to stop him. "I've never recommended canceling a trip, you know that. But you've got to pay the piper now or you're not going to get well. This is bad." I did not sign off on the plan. Doc went away and came back with Steve, who agreed I should cancel the trip. I did not agree. Doc went away and he came back with Steve and Jill. And I finally agreed — in part. I would not fly to Uruguay the next day, but I would fly to Guatemala City for the second part of the trip, which was the crucial part, after I took a couple of days to rest and heal.

I stayed put at the Naval Observatory that weekend, doing what business I could, but not feeling a whole lot better. I had a call with President-elect Tabaré Vázquez to apologize to him for missing his inauguration in Montevideo, and I had a call with President Poroshenko, who wanted me to know that, two weeks into the new ceasefire, the Russians had not yet stopped shelling across the border into Ukraine. Ukrainian soldiers and civilians were still being killed. And the international monitors could find no evidence that Russia was removing its heavy artillery from the front lines, as Putin had agreed to do. I told Poroshenko to stay strong and I would continue to do what I could to help. I also congratulated him on the anticorruption legislation his new government was going to pass next week, which would bring money from the IMF that was critical to stabilizing Ukraine's economy and protecting it from Putin's ongoing treachery.

Jill and I were upstairs in the private quarters for the first phone call from Houston with an update on Beau. The new scans looked bad, but the way I heard it, the doctors could not be sure if they were seeing new tumor growth or more necrosis, which is evidence of the destruction of the cancer cells. They said they would call as soon as they had more detailed information. I hung up and took a deep breath. Let it be necrosis, I said to myself. Please, God, let it be necrosis. They called us with the report later that night. The news could not have been worse. This was all new tumor growth. The cancer cells in Beau's brain were multiplying fast, and in new places. My heart sank.

This was the moment we had been dreading from the day Dr. Sawaya removed the original tumor.

Hunt got me patched into a separate conference call that weekend so the three of us — Beau, Hunt, and I — could all talk with Dr. Yung and Dr. Sawaya. The doctors explained the disconcerting architecture of the new growth. There was a large mass in front of the space where Dr. Sawaya had removed the original tumor. Sawaya was prepared to go in and remove it as soon as possible. But there was also growth well behind the original tumor, which Dr. Sawaya could not safely remove.

Dr. Yung told us there were other options for treatment and still reason for hope. Hunter thought maybe they could try the promising new experimental immunotherapy we had talked about a few months earlier. The medical team at M. D. Anderson had prepared Beau for the therapy a month earlier by drawing his blood and collecting some of his T cells — the white blood cells that identify and destroy malicious foreign agents in the body. The idea of this new immunotherapy was to identify the specific protein in the tumor cells that was triggering the growth and to engineer the patient's natural T cells to attack that specific protein only. The T cells would, in theory, gobble up the cancer cells and leave all the nearby healthy brain cells untouched. But it turned out they couldn't make that work. Beau's cancer cells had proven too diabolical; the doctors had been unable to identify and isolate the unique protein in Beau that was triggering the growth.

There was another possible treatment, Dr. Yung assured us, though it was further outside the box than anything they had tried to date. Dr. Sawaya would surgically remove the cancerous nodule in front and then, a few days later, another specialist at Anderson would inject a specially engineered live virus into the new tumor growth in the back. The purpose of the injection was to activate Beau's own immune system and let it attack the cancer cells. They had already had extraordinary success in a few of the twenty-five patients who had received the live virus injection. Dr. Yung explained that they also wanted to try something else in combination — a separate immunotherapy treatment designed to hypercharge the organic attack on the tumor. Beau would be the first person ever to have this combination, and the risk was enormous. There was the possibility that Beau's immune system would overreact and start eating healthy brain cells, too. Hunter asked most of the questions that day, because he knew what he was talking about and he could talk for Beau. I was a little lost sitting there listening to the medical jargon as the sleet pinged against the Observatory windows. I still felt lousy, and my head was swimming in all this talk of proteins and antibodies and antigens and reengineered viruses. I wasn't sure what the right course was, but Beau settled it. *All good. Let's do it. All good. All good.*

The surgery would have to wait three or four weeks, the doctors explained, to allow time for the chemotherapy drugs Beau was now taking to clear his system, so he would be able to heal after another major brain surgery. The doctors decided to do the first injection of the immunotherapy — called anti-PD-1 antibody — as soon as possible. Dr. Yung wanted to do the procedure in the middle of the next week, on Wednesday, March 4.

When I got off the phone, Jill and I just stared at each other, and embraced. At that moment, even in her embrace, I think I had lost hope. I was determined not to break down in front of Jill, since I knew it would really scare her. So I walked into the bedroom, grabbed my rosary, and started praying. I didn't know what to ask for, but the simple act of prayer calmed me. I had to be strong. I had to maintain my sense of hope. The real fight was on now. Beau had survived the early and middle rounds, but the decisive round was approaching fast, and we all had to gird up. This was life and death.

I knew Hunt would be going down to Houston to be with his brother for the first injection of the anti-PD-1 antibody, but I spent that Sunday night debating with myself what I should do next. The official plan at that moment was for me to get on a plane and make the trip to Guatemala the next morning, Monday, March 2. But I wanted desperately to stay home and be with Beau. What I really wanted to do was just go hold him. And I knew if I called Barack at the White House that night and told him why I was canceling my trip, he'd say, "Go, Joe. Take as much time as you need." But I also knew that nothing was going to happen with Beau while I was out of the country, and my canceling the trip would have only invited more attention to his circumstances. And besides, I'd be back on Wednesday morning before the first anti-PD-1 injection.

I also knew Beau would be disappointed

in me if I canceled, especially on his account. I had an obligation — a duty, Beau would call it — to the country. I have to admit, though, if it had been a different man in the White House that night — somebody whose policies and character I doubted — I might have made that call. I might have stepped away from my job for a time. But I felt an obligation to Barack, who was my friend. The president had put his trust and faith in me. He was counting on me. He had enough to worry about already without adding me to his list.

Jill and I got on the marine helicopter at 9:40 the next morning, flew to Andrews Air Force Base, and boarded Air Force Two for the flight to Guatemala City. I hadn't slept well and was still popping Mucinex and antibiotics. I couldn't take a deep breath without feeling a sharp stab in my left lung. But I was confident I was doing the right thing. I settled into my cabin and started reading through the briefing books.

I might have been in the minority even around the White House, but I really believed at that time that in terms of game changers for our long-term national security, Central America held the greatest potential for our administration. As so often happens, the opportunity grew out of a crisis, when thousands of children from the Northern Triangle — Guatemala, Honduras, and El Salvador — began showing up at our southern border in the summer of 2014. The influx of unaccompanied children captured the headlines as well as the imagination of the American people. What would cause that many parents to put their children on a bus and send them to America alone? What parent could imagine that was their best possible alternative? How bad did things have to be for those parents to put their children's lives at risk?

When Barack turned to me and said, *Joe, you've got to do something about this,* I was glad he had chosen me. It didn't take long for me to realize that we had a real chance to bend the arc of history a bit. In fact, of all the crisis spots around the world, I had come to believe that Central America held the best opportunity. With only two years left in office, we didn't have the time to get it right in most places. The best we were going to do in the Middle East was to maintain the line and start building the mechanisms among our allies to begin the long campaign of disabling and destroying ISIL and the other terrorist groups. Real stability in countries like Iraq, Libya, and Syria was a long way away. In eastern

Europe, all we could do was to keep building consensus to shame and isolate Putin and Russia. Maybe we could begin to lay down a foundation to make real progress with China. But I had come to believe we had a really good chance, if we were smart, and had lots of courage and a little bit of luck, to put our relationships in Latin America on an entirely hopeful new trajectory — one that turned the region from its inhabitants' widely held belief that the United States was the continental bully dictating policy to smaller countries, to the realization that we could be a true partner in improving those countries.

I had been saying it even before the unaccompanied-children crisis of 2014. I had first laid out some guiding principles for U.S. engagement in Latin America back in May 2013, at a speech at the State Department before a standing-room-only crowd, including dozens of diplomats and other government officials from across Latin America. "In the region, we're still viewed by many as disengaged, domineering, or both," I said, "but I would argue that's not us anymore. Too many in my country still look south to the region of 600 million people and see mostly pockets of poverty and strife. But that's not you anymore.

Neither stereotype is accurate. And they haven't been, I would argue, for some time.

"The changes under way give all of us an opportunity to look at the hemisphere in a very different way. . . . I think we should be talking about the hemisphere as middle class, secure, and democratic. From Canada to Chile and everywhere in between."

Central America was a critical link in ensuring that that became a reality. And my instinct was, after working closely with the presidents of Guatemala, Honduras, and El Salvador for the last nine months, that they believed I really meant it. That it was possible.

My old friend Tip O'Neill, the twentieth century's most colorful and successful Speaker of the House, famously said, "All politics is local." I've been around long enough to presume to improve on that statement. I believe all politics is personal, because at bottom, politics depends on trust, and unless you can establish a personal relationship, it's awfully hard to build trust. That is especially true in foreign policy, because people from different countries often know little about one another, and have little shared history and experience. I have spent countless hours trying to build trust across those divides, and I have always followed my father's advice: Never tell a man what his interests are. Be straight and open with him about your own interests. And try to put yourself in his shoes. Try to understand his hopes and his limitations, and never insist that he do something you know he cannot. It's really just about making the effort to make a personal connection.

Presidents Otto Pérez Molina of Guatemala, Juan Orlando Hernández of Honduras, and Salvador Sánchez Céren of El Salvador had become my friends in the last nine months. I believed they trusted me. I told the old communist guerrilla from El Salvador, President Sánchez Céren, "If I end up being in the jungle, I want to be with *you.*" And I was their contact. They knew I spoke for the president. I was their confidant. And I knew that if a new replacement suddenly showed up for the March 2015 summit, there was a chance the whole enterprise would suffer a serious setback. That was a chance I was unwilling to take.

I arrived in Guatemala City with a real tribute in hand — the possibility of a big new aid package for the Northern Triangle. I had put together a package that would take care of not only the security concerns of the three countries, but governance issues as well. I had worked with the State Department and my own staff, and with support from Republicans and Democrats in the House and the Senate we were able to develop an aid package similar to Plan Colombia, which had helped get Colombia on its feet. The billion-dollar package for the Northern Triangle was beyond anything they had ever seen or expected from the United States. The region could always count on the Republican-controlled Congress to put up a quarter of a billion dollars for drug interdiction, but the size and scope of this aid package was something entirely new. The budget request included money for police and security, sure, because these countries led the world in murder rates, but our administration's request balanced security and development assistance based on the key lesson from Plan Colombia: high-intensity law enforcement operations are not a long-term solution without a robust judiciary and strong government institutions.

The budget request, which had been presented to Congress in January, also included funding for boys' and girls' clubs to help keep at-risk youth from joining gangs; support to aid government agencies in collecting taxes more effectively and ensuring that those tax proceeds were managed fairly and transparently; and investment in regional energy integration to lower the incredibly high energy costs. The energy part was key, I believed. Lowering energy costs for the average citizen in the Northern Triangle could reduce inequality, promote economic growth, and even help cut down the levels of violence.

We were signaling fundamental changes in our relationship with the entire hemisphere. This was my fifth major trip in less than two years. President Obama was meanwhile about to normalize diplomatic relations with Cuba, which made it harder to demagogue about Yanqui imperialists. And when somebody in the administration stood up and said, "It's not what we can do for you, it's what we can do together," Latin America was starting to buy in. I had already been talking to my friends in the Senate, on both sides of the aisle, and I knew what was possible. So I could look each of the three Northern Triangle presidents in the eye and tell them that passage looked like a good bet. We might not get the entire billion, but we would get close.

By the time I went into the critical meeting of the trip — just the three Northern

Triangle leaders and me — I think they understood I was serious about helping them. But I told them they had to be serious about helping me help them. I would lobby the Hill to get the budget request passed, but there were things they had to do to reassure appropriators in the United States Congress. "First," I told them, "everybody up my way thinks you are all corrupt. Second, they think you don't deliver very well on your word. Third, your tax system and your regulatory schemes are corrupt. You collect almost no taxes from the wealthy, while soaking the poor and the meager middle class. So you've got to commit to making some changes."

They each knew from previous talks with me that I expected them to make some politically difficult promises. They each had to tackle the smuggling networks and correct the misinformation about the U.S. immigration system to stop the flow of immigrants across our southern border. They each had to be seriously committed to achieving the sort of governance that served *all* of their citizens. And they each had to match our aid package, and much more than dollar-for-dollar. I really challenged them to develop a serious plan and to start delivering results. If they did, I assured them, President Obama and I would meet their political will step by step. But if they couldn't step up, we wouldn't step up. I told them that if what I was asking was too difficult for them, I understood. No problem. I got it. But if they said yes, then I was going to go up to the Hill and make personal commitments, staking my credibility on their willingness to tackle internal reforms. I would be offering my assurance to Congress that things were going to be different down here. "If you don't live up to your promises," I said, "I'm going to be the guy who comes after you."

The private meeting with the three presidents was scheduled for fifteen or twenty minutes, but it lasted well over an hour. And we emerged with real purpose. The four of us spent the next several hours hammering out the inelegantly titled "Joint Statement by the Presidents of El Salvador, Guatemala, and Honduras, and the Vice President of the United States of America Regarding the Plan for the Alliance for Prosperity of the Northern Triangle." Molina, Hernández, Sánchez Céren, and I did not want to waste our time together. We took the unconventional tack of negotiating in real time, while our respective staffs scrambled back and forth behind us to agree on specific language.

The process was exhausting, but we came out with a document to reckon with. It had more than three dozen serious and specific commitments from the Northern Triangle presidents pledging to use the money and expertise we were offering to make sure their governments would actually be responsive to the needs of their citizens. There were specific commitments to provide access to quality education for the underserved; to empower women; to improve health care, nutrition programs, and public safety; and to reform the justice system top to bottom — from the police departments, to the courts, to the prison system. There were pledges to promote fairness in the tax system as well as efficiency and effectiveness in tax collections, and detailed plans to provide economic opportunity and affordable energy. The United States government would provide experts from our departments of Justice, the Treasury, Customs, and Energy to help the leaders of Guatemala, Honduras, and El Salvador set up mechanisms of governance that did not yet exist. I really believed these efforts could put the three countries on the road to political stability and the sort of broad economic expansion that benefited everyone.

All four of us — Presidents Molina, Hernández, Sánchez Céren, and me — signed the document and released it to the public. This was the crucial product of the trip, in black and white. I could present the statement to the members of Congress as proof of seriousness on the part of the Northern Triangle leaders, and proof of the accountability we had built into the agreement. My plan was to make it absolutely clear to Congress that I would not permit the State Department to release funds unless and until explicit granular commitments — such as hiring and training set numbers of teachers and cops in particular at-risk neighborhoods, or hitting targets on increasing tax revenues from the wealthiest of their citizens — had been executed. I would give my word that we would not write a check for any program until they had hit their mark on that program. I was going to put my credibility on the line in the halls of Congress, where members knew I had never broken a commitment.

I had a long heart-to-heart with my key staff in the main cabin of Air Force Two on the way back. There were a lot of obstacles that stood in the way of this plan actually working, I said to them, but I had been really impressed that the three Northern Triangle presidents seemed so willing to rise to the crisis at hand. I told the staff they had done a great job, but that there was a lot more to do when we got home. We had to start lobbying Congress for the appropriation, and we had to draw out more detailed commitments from the Northern Triangle leaders. We needed to align our assistance so that we were supporting both the short-term needs — like addressing the violence and the lack of opportunity in the most vulnerable communities — while also working patiently with the three countries on structural reforms and improved governance that could lead to real prosperity there.

It was nearing midnight on Tuesday and still below freezing in Washington when Jill and I arrived at the Naval Observatory. I had a hard time sleeping that night, thinking about Beau's first anti-PD-1 antibody injection, which was scheduled for the next day. Beau was still on my mind the next morning, at the office, as I filled in the president on what we had accomplished in Guatemala. I spent much of the day after that in my own office, waiting for the call from Houston about Beau's procedure. I was tired and worried and a little bit angry at the Fates. Why was this happening to my son? He just didn't deserve this. I glanced through the schedule for the rest of the week and was relieved to see that it didn't seem too taxing. It felt like I finally had some breathing room to focus on Beau. And then came the call from Haider al-Abadi. He was not an excitable man, but he was clearly in the middle of a serious crisis. "Joe," said the new prime minister of Iraq, "I need your help."

CHAPTER SEVEN: CALCULATED RISKS

Prime Minister Abadi needed serious military assistance in the new battle for Tikrit, he told me on the phone that day, March 4, 2015, and he needed it in a hurry. Abadi was in danger of losing control of a pivotal fight against the vicious new malignancy of terror growing in the Middle East, the Islamic State of Iraq and the Levant, or ISIL. His ask was a big one, consequential both to Iraq and to the United States. And beyond the global implications, this was an issue of great personal import to me. The majority of Americans had surely wearied of our costly twelve-year slog in Iraq, and many had tuned it out like so much annoying background noise. I could not. Having worked since 2003 to help build a functioning, inclusive government in Iraq that might develop into a real democracy, I was deeply invested. I had traveled to Iraq more than twenty times, first as ranking member and chairman of the Senate Foreign Relations Committee, and later as vice president, after Barack announced to me in a 2009 meeting of senior officials in the Oval Office, "Joe will do Iraq."

Iraq had arguably been the most frustrating issue of my forty-year career in foreign relations. Relations among the three main factions in Iraq — Shia Arabs, Sunni Arabs, and Kurds — were characterized by anger and paranoia, and punctuated by spasms of outright violence. The three factions nursed grudges both ancient and modern. The modern borders of the country were carved out of the Ottoman Empire following the first World War. Saddam Hussein's Baathist regime favored the country's Sunni Arab minority, while the aspirations of the majority Shia Arab population, concentrated in central and southern Iraq, and the Kurdish minority in the north were brutally repressed. The 2003 American invasion overturned this order, disenfranchising the Sunnis, empowering the Shia, and rekindling Kurdish dreams of independence. A dozen years trying to persuade the political leaders in Iraq to see the benefits of a government based on something other than raw power and sectarian dominance had been time-consuming, draining, and ultimately nearly impossible. But I wasn't ready to give up on it. Beau had risked life and limb serving a yearlong deployment in Iraq. He saw death and destruction there, though he didn't talk about it much. But he always insisted that what the United States was trying to do was noble. If there was a reasonable chance to get it right in Iraq — for the long term — Beau believed we should try. We had sacrificed too many good people already to give up. And on the day of Abadi's call, I thought we finally had a chance. The irony of all ironies was that the very outfit that intended to tear the country apart, ISIL, was actually bringing Iraqis together, at least temporarily.

The strength of ISIL in Iraq had caught not only the United States but the entire coalition by surprise in the summer of 2014, when its forces made a lightning offensive in the north and west of the country. ISIL fighters blew through the Iraqi security forces, gaining their first solid footholds in the extravagant and improbable project to create a repressive "Caliphate of the Islamic State" across the whole of the Middle East and then beyond. ISIL took almost a third of Iraq, most of it in the Sunni-majority areas. The group gorged itself on cash from banks it looted and on hundreds of millions of dollars' worth of sophisticated weaponry and equipment left on the battlefield when poorly commanded Iraqi units fled. ISIL terrorized the population with beheadings, mass executions, the burning and crucifixion of prisoners — and did it in public, recorded on video for all the world to see. It desecrated or destroyed Shia religious sites and libraries, and threatened minority Christian and Yezidi populations with genocide. ISIL menaced the oil-rich Kurdish stronghold of Kirkuk and took control of Iraq's second-largest city, Mosul, as well as Tikrit, the provincial capital of Salah ad Din.

The spread of ISIL's bloody rule changed the political calculus for all three factions in Baghdad, forcing them to think like the old American revolutionary Ben Franklin. "We must all hang together," Franklin had famously said, at the signing of the Declaration of Independence, "or assuredly, we shall all hang separately." My team used that moment of crisis to real advantage. I spent hours on the phone in 2014 — along with Ambassador Stuart Jones in Baghdad, Deputy Special Presidential Envoy Brett McGurk, and my national security team — trying to pry sufficient concessions from each faction to form the basis of an inclusive coalition government. Because the stubbornly sectarian policies of former prime minister Nouri al-Maliki helped give rise to ISIL, we worked like hell to negotiate the deal among the three factions that ultimately installed Haider al-Abadi, a Shia committed to a more inclusive government, as prime minister. After spending time with him and watching him work, I came to see Abadi as the single best shot at creating a true, working coalition government. He talked with me about his country becoming an anchor democracy in the Middle East. We agreed on the need for what he called "functioning federalism" — which meant allowing more autonomy to the separate provinces, some controlled by Sunnis and some by Kurds. And we spoke of the incredible economic potential of the country's enormous oil reserves. Iraq had more oil than Kuwait and Russia, and almost as much as Iran. Oil could be a boon fairly shared by all — the glue that could hold Iraq together.

We had worked right alongside Abadi to shape an Iraqi security force and a strategy capable of defeating ISIL — one that ensured that Iraqis stayed in the lead, so we could avoid sending tens of thousands of U.S. troops back into Iraq. The Maliki government had decimated the military and its command structure. Both would have to be rebuilt. Our military advisers helped Prime Minister Abadi identify Iraqi commanders he could appoint on the basis of competence, not religious sect. We tasked our Special Forces to assess which Iraqi units could actually be salvaged, helped them reconstitute their divisions, and began training new soldiers. We reequipped this new force with armored vehicles, ammunition, small arms, Hellfire missiles, and bomb detection technology.

When Abadi called me that morning in March 2015, a major operation against ISIL in Tikrit was just getting under way. And the prime minister made it clear to me on the phone that he was extremely worried about this unfolding assault. Tikrit was a flashpoint of sectarian grievance. Nine years earlier, violence between the Shia and Sunni in neighboring Samarra had tipped the country into a bloody civil war, and following ISIL's brutal killing of fifteen hundred air force cadets, many of them Shia, at a nearby Iraqi air base in June 2014, the prospect of a repeat was real. The operation to take the city had been planned — and was now being executed — outside the purview of the central government in Baghdad and outside the control of his minister of defense. A loose assortment of Shia militia groups known as the Popular Mobilization Forces (PMF) made up about three-quarters of the thirty-thousand-man attack; many were aligned with the government of Iran. Tehran seemed to be in the driver's seat of the operation. It had supplied artillery, tanks, drones, and military advisers. The most visible and well-known commander on the ground was Qasem Soleimani, head of Iran's notorious Islamic Revolutionary Guard Corps Quds Force. Soleimani was parading around the battlefield, flying an Iranian flag, taking selfies to be circulated in both Iran and Iraq. If the attack worked, Soleimani would be seen as the hero of Tikrit by much of the Shia population in the region, and the Iraqi government in Baghdad would be in debt to Iran. There would also be a dangerous precedent for a parallel security operation run by the Iranians in other places in Iraq. On top of that, Abadi feared that the violent reprisals by angry Shia fighters against Sunnis that were sure to follow the liberation of Tikrit would lead to escalating Sunni-Shia tensions that could splinter his tenuous new government.

We both knew that pushing ISIL out of Tikrit had to be done the right way, with the right forces. Abadi needed to gain control of the operation, and get his own Iraqi national troops in the lead, before it got out of hand. He needed help from the United States to do that, and he was counting on me to deliver. He asked for firepower from us to match or exceed Tehran's: drones to provide intelligence, surveillance, and reconnaissance (ISR); targeted air strikes from U.S. warplanes on ISIL fighters on the ground; additional ammunition and body armor; and U.S. advisers and planners to help coordinate the offensive. I still believed Abadi to be worthy of our help. I told him I would do what I could do, as fast as I could, but that there would have to be conditions attached to any American military assistance.

When the call came in from Houston that same day, the report was straightforward. The procedure to inject Beau with the anti-PD-1 antibody pembrolizumab — or pembro, as the doctors called it — had gone well. The procedure itself was a simple one. They put an IV into his arm, shot about 150 milligrams of pembro into his bloodstream over the next thirty minutes, and it was done. But as I stood in my office in the West Wing, I knew in my gut that little else would be simple in the coming months. We had crossed the medical Rubicon. The real fight was on now, for Beau and for our family. There was no telling how long it would last, because it was a novel fight in the history of glioblastoma treatment — a three-pronged attack on the cancer that had never before been executed in full. Dr. Sawaya would be performing the second risky maneuver, a surgery to excise the excisable part of Beau's tumor, at the end of March; as soon as Beau had healed from that operation, Dr. Frederick Lang would be injecting a specially engineered live virus into the remaining tumor. Then another injection of pembro a few weeks later, or as soon as Beau could handle it. At least, that was the plan.

The live virus itself was a relatively new treatment, developed by researchers and clinicians at M. D. Anderson over the previous fifteen years. The microbiology that underpinned the science of the treatment, however, dates back billions of years. Viruses have been around almost as long as living organisms, and the two have evolved on parallel, and sometimes crossing, tracks. Viruses are opportunists; they infiltrate and then manipulate living cells to their own ends. A virus invades normal human cells, knocks out the protein that prevents those healthy cells from dividing, and, using all the now-active division machinery of the host cell, starts making copies of itself. The doctors at M. D. Anderson were perfecting ways to put those malicious viral means to good ends. They had actually engineered a virus capable of destroying cancer cells while leaving healthy tissues untouched. This viral smart bomb, called Delta-24, lacks the ability to knock out the cell guardian protein, so it does no harm to healthy host cells. But a cancer cell does not have the gene that prevents the cell from dividing, so once Delta-24 has infiltrated a tumor, it uses the machinery of the already-dividing malignant cells to divide and replicate itself.

Delta-24 multiplies nonstop, until the cancer cell, glutted with expanding viral matter, explodes. The burst shoots viral particles into other nearby cancer cells and the process starts all over again. So Dr. Lang only had to inject one tiny spot and Delta-24 would, it was hoped, spread through Beau's entire tumor and destroy it in a series of cellular explosions. This particular virotherapy was an untested theory just a decade ago, and the doctors at Anderson could not rule out dangerous consequences back then. The first time a patient at M. D. Anderson was injected with a live virus, the doctor overseeing the procedure was too fretful to sleep that night. But the Anderson team was starting to have some success by the time Beau presented as a candidate for the Delta-24 injection. Dr. Lang had just finished the first major study, and he was encouraged and inspired by the results. Of the twenty-five patients in the study, there were three whose tumors had been blasted away. And those tumors had been large and recurrent, like Beau's was now. The treatment had extended those three lives by more than three years and Dr. Lang had detected a promising pattern in the successes. The live virus had induced an interesting reaction in the immune system of each of the three patients who had emerged tumor-free. Cancer cells have a way of eluding the detective force of the immune system, but a virus does not. The immune system recognizes the virus as foreign and attacks it. Delta-24, once it got into the cancer cells, appeared to have flipped a critical switch. The immune system had apparently begun to recognize the tumor proteins as foreign as well and started its own campaign to destroy the glioblastoma.

Lang and Yung were already considering

ways to boost the immune system separately while the live virus was also at work — and the best available was pembro, the anti-PD-1 antibody. Pembro was designed to help the immune system do what it could not do on its own: the drug would unmask the tumor as an unwelcome and dangerous foreign agent, and the body's own T cells would go to work to destroy it. Cancer cells put the brakes on the killer T cells. The anti-PD-1 antibody goes in and releases those brakes. Pembro had already been successful in treating melanoma and lung cancer, and the two doctors thought that using it on Beau might prove to be a real breakthrough in glioblastomas. Dr. Lang and Dr. Yung had both been clear about the risks when they laid out the plan to Beau and Hunter. The live virus alone could cause raging swelling in the brain, which could result in long-term damage or death. Even if it did work as hoped, Beau was likely to get much worse before he got better. The addition of the pembro increased the chances for complications. There were a lot of unknowns, Lang told them, because Beau was Patient Zero. Beau took it all in and looked over at Hunter, who was by his side for every consultation. Hunter appeared resolute, and Beau looked back at Lang and said, "Let me get it."

I found out only later that the medical professionals at Anderson had started to talk among themselves about Beau — how he never showed fear and never sagged. He wanted the doctors to throw everything at him they possibly could. He kept reassuring them that he could handle it. "We think we are brave if we go when we have a 50-50 chance of winning," the anesthesiologist who saw Beau at every one of his visits to Houston for twenty months said of my son. "True bravery is when there is very little chance of winning, but you keep fighting."

The first call I made after talking about Abadi with my national security adviser, Colin Kahl, and the rest of my team was to the U.S. military commander in charge of the Middle East, General Lloyd Austin. Austin was the heartbeat of Operation Inherent Resolve, our administration's six-month-old campaign to destroy ISIL. Working alongside our diplomats in the State Department, the general had already built a broad international coalition to counter ISIL, and he had shown a willingness to be aggressive on the battlefield. "My goal is to defeat and ultimately destroy ISIL. And if [ISIL] continues to present us with major targets," Austin had said soon after the first bombing campaigns began, "then clearly, we'll service those targets."

General Austin made it clear to me that he wanted to find a way to help Abadi, but he thought it unwise to provide air support and advisers to the operation in Tikrit in its current form. The chances were too great that U.S. or coalition air strikes would accidently hit Shia militiamen or their Iranian minders and spark an unnecessary conflict with Tehran. And he sure didn't want to be in the business of providing support for an Iranian-run operation. If Abadi wanted real help from the U.S. military, he was going to have to take charge of the operation, clear the field of the Shia militia units, and replace them with soldiers under his command.

By the time I sat down with President Obama to make the case for helping Abadi, I had begun to see the predicament in Tikrit as an opportunity. If the president set hard and fast conditions for our support, Abadi delivered, the Iraqis received the help they needed from us and pushed ISIL out of Tikrit, then the value of a unity government in Iraq would be apparent to all. Abadi would have passed his first real test. The conditions I suggested to the president were these: Before any U.S. air strikes began, command and control of the offensive would have to be shifted to Iraq's ministry of defense and Abadi himself, in coordination with the U.S.-led counter-ISIL coalition. We would need full visibility on all the forces on the battlefield and confidence that we knew exactly where every player was located, from the Shia militias, to Soleimani and his Iranian special forces, to the Iraqi army and federal police. The final attack to liberate the city had to be led by forces we trusted, including Iraq's elite counterterrorism services, the Iraqi army, and local Sunnis. The Iranian-backed militias had to withdraw to the outskirts of the city and remain there for the duration of the battle. Most important, there had to be a strong and visible contingent of Sunni tribal fighters in the final battle. And the Sunni civilians who had fled Tikrit during ISIL's rule or during this new battle had to be allowed to return to their homes in the city, with essential services like water and electricity to be restored and with the promise of protection from Shia reprisals.

The Sunni piece of the plan was critical for two reasons. First, it would prove that fighting ISIL in Iraq was not a war of Shia against Sunni, but a war of patriotic Shia,

Sunni, and Kurdish Iraqis against a dangerous and radical jihadist terror group. And second, it was the best hope to make peace and security in Tikrit (and other cities liberated from ISIL) sustainable for the long term. And unless peace and security were sustainable — militarily *and* politically, by the Iraqis themselves — there was no reason to risk a single American in the fight.

We had already lost 4,489 American lives in Iraq and spent more than a trillion dollars, with far too little gain to show for all that loss. President Obama was wary, as was I, about ending up with tens of thousands of American boots on the ground in Iraq, fighting another hot war. But if the operation in Tikrit worked as planned, it would likely set a template to be followed in future counter-ISIL operations there. When the fight turned to Mosul, the Kurdish commanders nearby would understand they needed to work with Abadi and his minister of defense in Baghdad in order to get U.S. military support. Iraqi soldiers (Shia, Sunni, and Kurd) under the command and control of Baghdad would do the fighting in their own theater, supported by U.S. airpower, planning, and training. And Iranian influence would be blunted. The president understood the risks, but he also understood the upside. We should communicate the conditions to Baghdad, he told me. The ball would be in Abadi's court.

Abadi did not hesitate when our ambassador presented the list of conditions in the middle of March; it came at just the right time for him. The battle for Tikrit was a stalemate. The Popular Mobilization Forces and the Iranian-backed elements on the ground had claimed control of about half of the city in the first week of attack, but they were no longer winning any new territory. ISIL soldiers, though badly outnumbered, were inflicting real damage. They had littered the ground with improvised explosive devices to slow attacks. ISIL suicide bombers roamed the streets in search of PMF targets. Casualties among the PMF grew to more than a hundred a day. Nearby morgues overflowed with the dead. "It's a furious fight," said one militiaman, who had just lost his father in the battle. "Harder than we thought."

The powers back in Iran, frustrated by the lack of progress, had begun to ship two-thousand-pound rockets and smaller missiles to the battlefield, raising concern that they were preparing a massive bombardment of the remainder of the city. "Generally speaking," one defense analyst told a

New York Times reporter, "these weapons are more effective at terrorizing civilians than providing fire support for ground operations." There were, meanwhile, unwelcome reports of Shia militiamen burning and looting Sunni homes and businesses in and around Tikrit. The fight appeared to be devolving into another Shia vs. Sunni sectarian brawl, a brawl that could blow apart Abadi's government.

So the prime minister decided to use our conditions as I had hoped he would — as an opportunity to seize the reins. Abadi made the formal request for the air strikes and other aid from the U.S.-led coalition, explained to the Iraqi parliament the dire need of U.S. assistance, and then started checking off the boxes. He handed command and control to his minister of defense, a Sunni Muslim; sent his elite counterterrorism services to Tikrit to be the point of the spear in the attack; brought more Sunni tribesmen into the fight; ordered the Shia militia units to stand down in Tikrit; and reassured leaders of Sunni governments in Saudi Arabia, Egypt, and Jordan that security in the Sunni city, once liberated, would be handled by local Sunni police and not by outside Shia militiamen who might still be nursing understandable malice.

Abadi had a hard time selling this new plan to the majority Shia party in the Iraqi parliament, but he got crucial political cover from the spiritual leader of Iraq's Shia Muslims. On March 20, 2015, Ayatollah Ali al-Sistani sent a representative out at Friday prayer in Karbala to express the necessity for national unity in the battle for Tikrit — which meant Shias fighting side by side with Sunnis to expel ISIL. The minute I saw the statement from Sistani's man I knew Abadi had cracked the code; it increased my faith in Abadi's strategic ability as well as his political instincts.

The first American air strikes began to hit ISIL targets on March 25, 2015. Predictably, a few of the Iranian-sponsored Shia militia leaders expressed displeasure as the bombing began. "Some of the weaklings in the army say that we need the Americans," said one Popular Mobilization Force commander, "but we say we do not need the Americans." Other Shia militiamen announced that they were picking up their weapons and going home. A few said they were sticking around in hopes of finding Americans to attack. The most telling sign, however, was the retreat of Soleimani. The Iranian Quds Force commander realized he had lost his opportunity to claim victory in Tikrit on behalf of Iran. He'd been outmaneuvered and had no option but to return to Tehran. The show of American airpower reset the battlefield inside Tikrit. "The hour of salvation" had arrived, Abadi announced that evening on Iraqi state television. "We will liberate each inch of Iraq. The victory of Iraq is being achieved by Iraqis, hero Iraqis," he said, "with support from friendly countries and the international coalition."

I felt good that day, as the new battle began to unfold. ISIL still held more than half of the city, but Abadi had gained control of the operation. And we had given his forces a fighting chance. What would happen from here was no sure thing. I agreed with the assessment offered to a reporter on the ground in Iraq by an unnamed U.S. official: "This was a calculated risk," he said, "but it's one that had to be taken."

The day after the air strikes began in Tikrit, I boarded an unmarked plane with my family for a trip to M. D. Anderson Cancer Center in Houston. Beau would be there for a week at least, to undergo the surgery and then the injection of the live virus. At Beau's request, we were all working hard to ensure his privacy, which required remarkable acts above and beyond the call of duty by a number of people — most crucially, our Secret Service detail. While I had always greatly admired and respected them, over the course of the previous eighteen months I had developed a new appreciation for the men and women on my detail. The team had shown kindnesses to my family that were well beyond professional and were impossible to repay. I occasionally heard one of the agents say that they were here to protect more than our bodies; they were determined to protect our dignity. And I had become increasingly aware of that in the last few months, especially during our recent family outings, when agents would surreptitiously step in front of citizen photographers to make sure they didn't get any pictures of Beau's obvious physical decline. Or how they would hang back at the top of the trail in the Tetons so Beau, Hunter, and I could have a moment of privacy, just the three of us, at the top of a mountain.

I had also come to rely on my new personal aide, Colonel John Flynn. Flynnie was an air force pilot — he flew C-17s — who had been one of my military aides when Beau was first in trouble. The colonel had taken it upon himself back in August 2013 to figure out how to get the entire family to and from M. D. Anderson without inviting attention. He called friends he could trust in the air force, got a flight pattern and a secured remote airfield where we could land, and he did it all without causing any chatter inside the military. And Colonel Flynn, who had become a very close friend by then, made it happen again on March 26. We flew to Ellington Air Force Base and took a loose and quiet motorcade — no motorcycle cops, no sirens — right to a side entrance at the hospital complex, barely visible from the main roads.

From the moment we all walked into the hospital, I was reminded of how the people at M. D. Anderson had become something like extended family. And it wasn't just Dr. Yung and Dr. Sawaya. The hospital had a special envoy who always made sure Beau got in and out of all his tests and procedures with minimal hassle and absolute privacy. He met us as we entered the facility and it was obvious Beau, Hallie, and Hunter knew him well — "Hey, Chris!" — and counted on his help. He was a friend. He escorted us up to Dr. Yung's office, where the advanced practice nurse, Eva Lu Lee, who did the intake, gave Beau a big hug and a kiss, and asked after Natalie and Hunter. "Beau," she said, pointing to his green socks, "I see you're wearing them again." She was a friend. Dr. David Ferson, the anesthesiologist who had been the other crucial physician in Beau's awake craniotomy in 2013, made sure to be at Beau's preoperative scan in the MRI area. The scans took a long time, and Beau was encased deep in the small machine during the procedure. Dr. Ferson knew Beau was uncomfortable and slightly claustrophobic, so he always made sure to be on hand to help out. He was a friend, too.

Jill and I felt better seeing how many reinforcements our son had here at Anderson. And we were reminded again of the incredible support Beau was getting from the entire family. Hallie was still a rock, even in the face of her husband's obvious physical deterioration. Ashley was there to be with her big brother, and Ashley's husband, Howard, an M.D. himself, had stayed in constant contact with the doctors at Anderson, talking over treatment and keeping an eye on Beau for them in the long intervals between visits. Howard also translated the medical talk into plain English for me. But the more I saw and heard at Anderson, the clearer it became to me that Hunter Biden was the crucial beam in Beau's support structure. His mission, Hunter had confided to Dr. Yung, was to save his brother. And Hunter's determination, I knew, was a real act of bravery. I had always tried to impart to my children the lesson that my mother taught me, my sister, and my brothers: There is no one in the world you are closer to than your brother and sister. You have to be able to count on each other.

Hunt understood the Biden code from the time he was a kid. He could be counted on. He was the person at the front of the wedge in the hallways, out ahead of the Secret Service agents, making sure Beau got where he was going on time. He pulled Dr. Yung aside separately to ask the questions that might have answers he would want to shield from Beau. Hunt was at the scans, standing at the corner of the MRI machine, so he could rub Beau's foot and talk to him, to keep him calm. Whatever Beau asked for — water, fruit, a sandwich — Hunter *ran* for it, so his brother did not have to wait. He sat with Beau in the hotel room in the downtimes, watching golf. He made a trip to the gift shop to buy a new multiday pillbox to help manage the growing regimen of drugs. "Hunt, I already have a system," Beau argued. "I know what I'm doing." But Hunt was not going to let him make a mistake. "I'm going to *make sure* you're doing it," he insisted. Hunt crawled into bed with Beau just to be near, so Beau could talk. And Hunt was there to put his arms around Beau in the moments before his brother went into surgery.

The entire scene at Anderson would have been encouraging, but for one big thing: while Beau was still determined and mentally tough, he did not seem physically well to me. He came through the surgery on March 27 just fine, with no ill effects to his cognition or his motor skills. Dr. Sawaya had excised all he had hoped to, but the tumor appeared to be growing fast now, and Beau was weak. The medical team had decided to wait until the next Thursday, April 2, to do the injection of the live virus. That was still six days away. But Dr. Yung and Dr. Lang wanted to be sure Beau was strong enough to handle it. So all we could do now was wait.

The family spent most of the next forty-eight hours at Beau's bedside making sure he was comfortable, or consulting with Dr. Yung, or sitting around our hotel rooms trying to remind one another in spoken and unspoken ways that there was still hope. Our job was to keep that flame alive, and to make sure Beau *felt* it. Hallie was anxious and exhausted, but she never showed it. She insisted on spending the night with Beau in his hospital room instead of going up to her hotel room. She spent hours rubbing his feet, telling him he was going to get through this.

The White House Communications Agency had installed a secure telephone line in a room near Beau's so I could deal with any emergencies that only I could handle. The most important call on my schedule was the day after Beau's surgery, March 28, with Prime Minister Abadi. I had a fifteen-minute briefing with my national security team and officials from the State and Defense Departments that Saturday morning, and was on the phone with Abadi by ten o'clock.

He sounded better that morning. The battle for Tikrit was gaining momentum. Abadi's troops were advancing toward the center of the city from four separate directions. U.S. airplanes and drones had carried out eighteen separate air strikes that day and had reportedly "pulverized" eleven of ISIL's key fighting positions. But the battle was getting tougher — house-to-house warfare in dense residential neighborhoods. ISIL fighters were constantly regrouping to defend smaller pockets in the city; they set houses on fire or left them booby-trapped. Abadi wanted more drones in the air to provide intelligence for his own soldiers, as well as more air strikes. He also pointed out that ISIL was exploiting the Iraqi government's focus on Tikrit to turn up the heat in Anbar Province, including in the contested city of Ramadi, which was less than two hours by car from downtown Baghdad.

My charge on the phone that day, as I saw it, was to express faith in my friend and remind him of what he had already accomplished. There was plenty of good news to build on: Abadi had convinced the Shia militias and their Iranian sponsors to back away from front lines. Abadi's commanders on the ground were showing real ability, and had apparently persuaded local Sunni fighters to buy into the operation. I applauded his Iraqi security forces for showing real courage and real grit. The battle was far from over, but the big message I wanted to convey to Abadi was that the president and the U.S. military were still behind him, and so was I.

I got off the phone with Abadi thinking this operation just might work, but aware that the outcome was largely out of my hands at this point. *This just might work* was a phrase that seemed to define my entire life at the moment. Keeping the faith about Tikrit, like keeping the faith about Beau, was an act of will — a kind of house-to-house fight against doubt. I crawled into bed that night, said my rosary, and then made a special plea to Neilia and my mom: "Please. Please. Look out for Beau. And give me the strength to handle whatever happens."

Two days after his surgery Beau was stable. There seemed to be no ill effects from the surgery. He was up and walking; his spirits were high. He was well enough that we decided it was okay to fly home for a few days and come back for the injection of the live virus on April 2. Hunt insisted on staying behind with his brother.

Leaving Beau in Houston was hard, though. I visited his room on my way out of town to tell him I would be back on Thursday for the injection of the live virus, and to let him know I was proud of him. "Honey, you're doing an incredible job," I told him. "And the science is with us. It's really moving fast. We're going to beat this damn thing. You and Hunt and I have a lot to do. We have a lot of life to live."

"It's all good, Dad. All good."

Then I put on my sunglasses and a ball

cap and we all sneaked out a side door for the drive to Ellington. As Air Force Two took off, I felt compelled to open up my diary and write: *March 29 — Leaving MD Anderson with hope. Beau is an amazing man. As is Hunter. He is staying with [Beau] until the next procedure. I'll be coming back.* I paused. What else was there to say? I was afraid if I really opened up, I would give into a lurking despair, and I could not allow that to happen. I could not allow Beau or anyone else to see that, ever. I set aside the diary until the flight was nearly over, then picked it up again to add one line. *Just landed. 6:07. I feel so goddam lonely.*

The president's office rang right on schedule, the first day of April 2015, and I grabbed my notes and headed down the corridor to the Oval Office for my weekly lunch with Barack. We had something worth celebrating. Haider al-Abadi was the big news all morning; there were television feeds and photographs of the prime minister walking down the streets of Tikrit, surrounded by a parade of Iraqi counterterrorism servicemen, federal police, Sunni tribal fighters, and a smattering of Shia militiamen. Some of the photos showed Abadi carrying a flag with three separate horizontal stripes — red, white, and black — emblazoned with green lettering in Arabic reading, ALLAHU AKBAR, or "God is great." The Iraqi national flag. The militia flags appeared to have been stowed away. "Our heroic forces have entered the center of Tikrit and raised the Iraqi flag," Abadi told the crowd of soldiers, civilians, and reporters. His defense minister back in Baghdad, Khalid al-Obeidi, was trumpeting the fall of Tikrit to the entire country. Iraqi soldiers, federal police, and Sunni fighters had done the hard house-to-house combat to clear the city of the last of the ISIL fighters, with a real assist from U.S. pilots, advisers, and weaponry. ISIL was finished in Tikrit, and its aura of invincibility had been punctured. "We have the pleasure, with all our pride, to announce the good news of a magnificent victory," said Obeidi. The citizens of Tikrit had been rescued, and the defense ministry in Baghdad was just getting started, Obeidi assured — next up was Mosul to the north, and then on to the ISIL-controlled cities to the west. "Here we come to you, Nineveh!" Obeidi said. "Here we come to you, Anbar!"

The president and I talked briefly about Tikrit at our lunch, and about what might come next in Iraq, but I think he could tell

I was distracted and down. He knew I was just back from M. D. Anderson, and he knew I was headed back there soon. The president had kept up with the general outlines of what had been happening in Houston.

"How did it go, Joe?" he asked. "How is Beau?"

The talk at lunch ended up being almost entirely about Beau. I could tell looking at him across the table that the president was genuinely concerned. He liked Beau and respected him and thought, like me, that my son had a big future ahead of him. I found myself explaining to him what Beau had just been through the previous week and what was coming up, attempting to keep it on a fairly straightforward, clinical footing. Part of that was for my own protection. I did not want to break down in front of anybody, least of all the president of the United States. The one time I had cried in front of other people, in the hours after Beau had that first strokelike episode three years before the cancer diagnosis, I remember feeling ashamed afterward. I determined then to never, ever let that happen again other than with family. And I had lived up to that. But as I talked to Barack across the table that day I must have started to confide things I hadn't intended to. I was hurting, and the president could see it. As I explained to him that the next procedures were uncharted territory, but they were our only hope to save Beau, I looked up and found Barack in tears. He is not a demonstrative man, in public or in private, and I felt bad. I found myself trying to console him. "Life is so difficult to discern," he said.

I told him I was debating whether to fly down to Houston later that night, to be with Beau for the injection in the morning, or to fly tomorrow and be there when he woke up. Barack didn't hesitate. He said I should be with my son *before* he went in, not after. Whatever was on my schedule could not be more important.

"Joe," he said, "you've got to go down tonight."

I knew he was right. That's what I had planned on doing, but it meant something to me to hear it from Barack. I was in the air, heading to Houston, a few hours later.

CHAPTER EIGHT:
HOME BASE

Sunday, April 12, was the sort of day when all good things seem possible. Jill and I woke up at our home in Wilmington and the sun was already starting to burn away the last wisps of fog on the lake behind our house. Early lilacs were blooming, and even the tallest trees around the lake were leafing out. It felt like the dark gloom of a very difficult winter was finally lifting. Jill and I were looking forward to spending most of the day with our youngest grandchildren, Natalie and Hunter. Beau and Hallie were bringing them over later that morning to tape a segment for *Reading Rainbow*'s "Story Time." Natalie, Hunter, Jill, and I were all going to be reading from Jill's children's book, written for the families of U.S. military personnel who had been deployed overseas. At heart, it was the story of how Natalie and Hunter coped with the difficulty of having their dad far away, in a dangerous spot, for more than a year.

Everyone arrived, and while the crew spent the morning setting the lights in our library, we reviewed the parts each of us was to read: *"Daddy is a soldier,"* Natalie's *mom answers in a quiet voice. . . . "Soldiers have to do hard things sometimes." Her father takes Natalie in his arms. "Home is wherever I'm with you," he sings softly. Natalie smiles. "I like that song, Daddy."* The sun was up high by the time Natalie, Hunter, Jill, and I sat down in our library to tape the segment, and it was warm enough to throw open the doors that led out onto the back porch.

Beau kept to himself that day, out of sight of the visiting television crew, but I only had to walk twenty feet, through a couple of doors, to check in on him. He was settled into our sunroom, windows pushed open, where he could look down on the lake and feel the gentle, warm breeze on his face. This was his favorite spot in our house, where I sometimes found him sitting quietly on nice days like today, watching the play of light and shadow on the water as a single cloud or two scudded by overhead. Below was the dock where he had spent hours with his son, their fishing lines dangling in the water. Overhead in the distance, he would spy an egret or two making long, lazy arcs before turning and gliding down to skim the still surface of the lake. Jill always said we were going to will our property to Beau, he loved it so much. We could find ways to even things out for Hunt and Ashley, she said, but Beau should have the house.

Our eldest son was holding his own against the cancer. Was better than holding his own. He had come through the injection of the live virus ten days earlier without a single complication. He was moving well. His appetite was still good. And he was mentally sharp. But the two fresh, angry scars on his scalp put us all on edge; the entire family was dreading the coming effects of the untested experimental treatment. Dr. Yung and Dr. Lang had warned us that Beau would get worse before he got better. Maybe much worse. They said he would likely be at his most vulnerable point in the third or fourth week, when the virus and Beau's own immune system were at war with the tumor. The inflammation could be painful and debilitating. There was no predicting how low he would get, or if he would survive the onslaught. The climb up from the physical nadir could take a long time, too, and we wouldn't know for sure until then if the treatment had been successful and Beau's tumor was gone. The next six or eight weeks would tell all.

Beau was still determined, but I could tell he was tired. And he needed to gather some strength for his trip back down to M. D. Anderson in two days. He was going to have another set of scans, and if all looked good, he would get the second injection of pembro, the anti-PD-1 antibody. Howard had been on the phone with Dr. Yung about the wisdom of the second shot. Beau's immune system could potentially jump the tracks and start eating away healthy brain tissue. The doctors were still debating among themselves. Beau was ready to take the risk. He knew just how bad this could get, but he was willing to face it, and I think in large part, he was willing to face it for the rest of us. He had texted a friend two days earlier with an assessment of how things were going. "All good!"

I was the last of the four to read from Jill's book at the taping: "Natalie and Hunter are playing soldier with their Daddy dolls. Hunter starts to cry." I suddenly realized this was not going to be easy to get through. The absence of the father felt too close to home, too close to this home.

" 'I want Daddy.' Natalie holds her doll up in front of her face. She pretends the doll is a puppet. 'Don't cry, Hunter. Be a big and strong boy,' she says in her Daddy voice.

" 'That's not Daddy talking,' says Hunter.

" 'Yes, it is. That's what Daddy would say.' "

When we finished the taping, I went back to the sunroom and found Beau sitting with my sister, Val. They were flipping through news channels and looking over the newspapers. The big story that Sunday was Hillary Clinton, who had officially announced her candidacy for the Democratic presidential nomination. The chatter on cable news among pundits and professional prognosticators was that her announcement all but sealed the deal. She was a lock for the nomination. They pointed to her fifty-point lead in the early polls over her strongest challenger, me. Lesser-known candidates like Vermont senator Bernie Sanders were polling below 3 percent. President Obama had offered what seemed like a co-ordinated, nonendorsement endorsement the day before. "She was a formidable candidate in 2008," the president told reporters while on a trip to Panama. "She was a great supporter of mine in the general election. She was an outstanding secretary of state. She is my friend. I think she would be an excellent president." This was on the heels of a meeting I'd had with the president's trusted pollster earlier that week, a meeting I had taken at the president's urging. The message I took from that meeting was that Hillary's poll numbers, her money, and her campaign organization were just too formidable. I had no real path to the nomination, so why rock the boat and complicate things for the party?

None of that mattered to Beau. He was reading all he could about the Clinton campaign — its message, its candidate's travel schedule, its early field operation. He wanted to be up on everything, so he would be ready to pitch in the minute I announced my own candidacy. Beau believed, as I did, that I was prepared to take on the presidency. That there was nobody better prepared. No matter what people in the outside world said or thought, Beau and Hunter believed we could win. In my own head, the race was more than anything a matter of daring. And if I had my two sons behind me, anything was possible. Beau had a way of instilling courage and calming me. He was the last person in the room with me before the presidential primary debates in 2007, the vice presidential debate in 2008, and the vice presidential debate in 2012, when it was up to me to put wind back in the Democrats' sails after Barack's demoralizing performance in his first debate against Mitt Romney. Beau would always grab my arm just before I walked onstage and pull me back toward him until I was looking into his eyes. "Dad. Look at me. Look at me, Dad. Remember, Dad. Home base, Dad. Home base." What he was saying was: Remember who you are. Remember what matters. Stay true to your ideals. Be courageous. Then he would kiss me and shove me forward. So the 2016 Biden campaign would have a late start. So what? If Beau made it through the next few months and came out alive, I *knew* we could do this.

I was in the office three days later, that Wednesday, when the call came from Houston. My brother Jimmy had made the trip with Beau down to M. D. Anderson so Dr. Yung and Dr. Lang could assess the early results of the live virus injection, and Dr. Yung could administer the second injection of pembro. The news as it was reported to me was very good. In fact, the news was potentially incredible. The scans showed inflammation, but it looked like the tumor growth had really slowed. There was clear evidence of necrosis on the edge of the tumor, which meant the virus was probably already exploding cancer cells. Beau was in good shape, not yet showing ill effects from the virus, and there was already evidence of tumor destruction. This was something they hadn't seen in nearly three dozen tries with the live virus injection. I asked if it was because of the earlier pembro treatment. "That's what we're hoping," Dr. Yung said.

I got on the phone with Howard and with my brother Jimmy. Howard said Dr. Lang and Dr. Yung were excited by the possibilities. Jimmy was even more bullish. The doctors had never done this before, but they were very encouraged. *We really may have something* was the way Jimmy heard it. *We may have cracked the atom.* "Lang and Yung are almost giddy," my brother told me. I hung up the phone and felt like I could take a real, long, deep breath for the first time in months. Don't get your hopes too high, I reminded myself. Don't tempt the Fates.

Dr. Yung was concerned about being overly aggressive. The tumor had been growing fast just two weeks earlier, and Yung and Beau had agreed to fight it with like aggression. But now that the tumor seemed to be slowing in its growth, or maybe even shrinking, and Beau was in pretty good shape, Dr. Yung was leaning toward caution. He told Beau they could wait another couple of weeks, take another set of scans, and see if he needed another injection of pembro then. Both Yung and Lang were a bit surprised at Beau's reaction to pumping the brakes. He seemed to shrink into himself a little bit when he got the news. By the time he got home to Wilmington late that night, he was downhearted, though he never showed it. When Jimmy dropped him home, Beau gave him the thumbs-up. "All good, Uncle Jim. Hundred percent. All good."

Beau didn't get out of bed the next day, Thursday, and everybody in the family figured it was just exhaustion from the trip. But he didn't get out of bed on Friday, either. He was overwhelmed by fatigue and wouldn't eat. Howard stopped by Beau's house on Saturday and found him lethargic and unresponsive. He was certain Beau was badly dehydrated. Beau didn't want to go to the hospital, so Howard gave him three liters of fluids to boost his electrolytes. When Howard came back the next day and found him worse, he packed Beau off to Thomas Jefferson University Hospital in Philadelphia. This was likely the start of the first serious symptoms of the virus. Beau was still badly dehydrated when they admitted him, and his sodium levels were dangerously low. He couldn't keep his eyes open. He was barely responsive. The best he could do in response to a question was a thumbs-up, or a barely audible "Yes."

This was it now. We were in the worst of it, and unsure how long the worst would last. The effects of the virus were beginning to punish Beau. The swelling in his brain was intensifying and the pain would have been excruciating, so the doctors kept him heavily sedated most of the time. There was a lot of talk in Wilmington about why Beau, who had announced his intention to run for governor, had skipped every crucial political event in the first four months of the year. Beau still wanted to keep his illness out of the public eye. He was admitted to Jefferson under the same alias he had gone by at Anderson, "George Lincoln." The Secret Service agents kept going out of their way to ensure Beau's privacy and to protect his dignity. I would visit when I could sneak in and out without detection, but I made sure to keep up my schedule so I didn't call attention to his hospitalization.

So I wasn't around as much as I wanted to be, which was every moment, but Howard and Doc O'Connor agreed to be my eyes and ears at the hospital. Howard ran over to the ICU whenever he had a spare moment. Doc sat in the room during visiting hours when Hallie or other members of the family were there, and played the M.D. card to gain entrance to Beau's room in the off-hours to sit with him. Howard and Doc phoned me with reports as often as they could. Beau was under heavy sedation around the clock and rarely conscious. Occasionally nurses would give him something to wake him up, and he would give a thumbs-up — his nonverbal *All good!* — when they asked him how he felt.

Whenever I mused out loud to Doc that maybe I should dump my schedule and just move in to Jefferson, he would caution that we were in for a long haul. The prime minister of Japan was coming to town, and I had to deliver an important speech at the NAACP meeting in Detroit, and Natalie was bringing her entire class on a field trip to the White House and then for pizza back at the Naval Observatory. Doc reminded me that we weren't sure how long it was going to take for Beau to climb out of this, so I had to be patient and keep hitting my marks. "Nothing is happening right now, but I'll let you know the minute it does," he kept saying, "and we can get you up here in no time if we need to."

Somebody from the family was at Beau's bedside constantly, and other good friends stopped by to lend support. One of the visitors was Michael Hochman, a college friend of Beau's who had a present for him. Right after Beau's diagnosis in August 2013, the two of them decided to run a marathon, something neither had ever done. They trained on the hilly trails in Brandywine State Park together, all through the fall and winter. Beau was still as competitive as ever, even sick, pushing Michael. But over time Beau was only capable of a slow jog, and then a walk. He encouraged his friend to keep going without him, though, and he did. Michael showed up at Beau's bedside the last week in April, having just completed the Kentucky Derby Festival Marathon. Beau was not really able to talk and just barely awake during the visit. But Michael told him about the race. "We did it, Beau," he said, and put the finisher's medal on his chest. Beau squeezed his arm. "The medal is more his than mine," Michael said to Val, who was staying with Beau that day. "He was the wind at my back."

I don't remember telling Barack about Beau's hospitalization, but he must have sensed something was afoot. He let me know he was thinking of me in the way it was most comfortable for him. He seemed to be going out of his way to say nice things about me in public, especially in my absence. When he hosted the winners of the 2014 NASCAR Sprint Cup Series at the White House two days after Beau's hospitalization, he spoke about the teamwork required to win championships, and how their success reminded him of his relationship with me. "Instant chemistry," he called it. "When you have a trusted partner shouting world-class advice into your ear at every turn, you can't lose." The president made an unusually fond statement about me at the White House Correspondents' Dinner later that week, though he wrapped it in a joke about the then-current controversy involving businesses that had refused to cater to gay weddings. "I tease Joe sometimes," Barack said, "but he has been at my side for seven years. I love that man. He's not just a great vice president, he's a great friend. We've gotten so close, there's places in Indiana that won't serve us pizza anymore."

Beau's illness made me increasingly aware of the incredible advances and the new possibilities in cancer treatment, but I had also become painfully aware of the unnecessary snags and obstacles in our health-care system. We had an extraordinary team of doctors at Anderson and at Jefferson who were absolutely dedicated to saving Beau, but we still had frustrations — right from the beginning. The doctors who administered Beau's radiation treatments at Jefferson, for instance, did not readily accede to the idea of taking orders from a doctor at another hospital, even though we had made it plain that we had chosen Al Yung, at M. D. Anderson, to quarterback Beau's treatment. It was only after Howard explained to the radiologists at Jefferson that they *would* listen to Dr. Yung, or Beau would go elsewhere for his treatment, that they agreed.

Howard was an incredible secret weapon for Beau, and something all families should have: a devoted patient advocate. He acted as a translator between the doctors, who tend to speak in almost incomprehensible professional jargon, and Beau, Hallie, Hunter, and the rest of our family. Howard also did what he could to cut through the knotty administrative issues all families must face. One of the biggest problems was simple communication and information sharing between hospitals. The economic recovery package our administration pushed through in 2009 included nearly twenty *billion* dollars to aid hospitals and doctors' offices across the country to implement and update their electronic medical records system. The problem was, the system upgrades lacked uniform software. There were a handful of very capable and ingenious vendors servicing major healthcare providers, and they each had proprietary technology. Which meant the various systems were unable to talk to one another. (Read: their creators were unwilling to make them talk to one another.) One of our biggest frustrations during Beau's time in the Philadelphia hospital was the inability of the doctors and technicians at M. D. Anderson to interface with the doctors and technicians at Jefferson. Dr. Yung and Dr. Lang needed to see the scans in real time, but the two hospitals were on two different systems, so Anderson was unable to receive electronic files of the scans of Beau's brain they were doing at Jefferson. Nobody wanted to lose the valuable time waiting for the arrival in the mail of a physical CD, so Howard and Hunter were forced to get on FaceTime with Dr. Yung and use the cameras on their iPads to stream images from Philadelphia to Houston. This, I determined at the time, was something that needed fixing.

Beau held steady for ten or twelve days, and there was some evidence on the scans that the tumor might be shrinking. His appetite was still bad, so the doctors inserted a feeding tube. But in the first few days of May, he started showing a little improvement. He was more responsive, and the nurses even got him out of bed and helped him take his first steps in almost two weeks. Late one afternoon when I was with him and he was awake, we were talking to one of the nurses. "Where do you live?" I asked her. She pointed out the window, across the Delaware River; the sky was the beautiful after-light that follows a warm spring rain. "I live right over there," she said, pointing. "Oh, look at the rainbow! Look at the rainbow. Where it landed. My house is right there." Then she turned to Beau. "It's good luck, Beau," she said. "That's good luck." I took that rainbow as a sign. If Beau was on the upswing, we decided he should go to Walter Reed, the military facility just outside Washington, where he would be able to restart his physical, speech, and occupational therapy once he rebounded from this temporary, virus-induced illness.

When "George Lincoln" arrived at Walter Reed on May 5, 2015, a team was already in place for his rehab. He got visits that first day from a nutrition counselor, a speech therapist, and an endocrinologist who was going to watch his salt level over the next few days. And they helped him dodge a potentially deadly bullet. A very observant resident who stopped in to see him noticed that Beau seemed to be suffering real discomfort; it turned out to be peritonitis, an infection in his abdomen where his feeding tube had accidently pulled loose. He was rushed into emergency surgery to replace the feeding tube and clean out the infection. Complications piled up for the next two weeks and brought him more suffering and more pain. He was courageous and stoic, and just kept fighting, but every time Beau looked to be gaining ground, something would knock him back. The oxygen tube that fed through his mouth was agonizing for him, so a surgeon performed a tracheostomy and inserted a breathing tube at the base of his neck. He was just barely responsive for long stretches, and his entire right side was nearly paralyzed. There was fluid buildup in the left ventricle of his brain, and every time the doctors drained it the fluid just came back, which meant he was in pain or disoriented when he was conscious. One night, at two o'clock in the morning, his breathing suddenly became labored, which turned out to be a sign of pneumonia, requiring a jolt of powerful antibiotics. When a Catholic priest swung by Beau's room to check in, Jill thanked him for stopping by but asked him to please leave. And not to come back. She didn't want Beau to get the idea he was there to perform last rites. In fact, there would be no discussion about last rites.

Jill and I kept reminding each other the doctors had warned us that Beau would get much worse before he got better. We kept telling ourselves that these hard times were to be expected, and he would turn the corner. Could be any day now. There was still hope.

What I felt, most of all, was helpless. I did what I could, which was to just be there whenever I could. I visited early in the morning most days, before I started my official schedule, and again every night when I was done. The ride to the hospital was less than half an hour from the White House, and even faster from our residence at the Naval Observatory. Once the motorcade hit the hospital grounds and made the left into the back alley, I would always look up at Beau's room on the second floor to see if the light was on. Maybe he's up tonight, I'd think. Maybe he's looking out the window at me. The agents would let me out of the car at a side door, where I would be met by an army nurse, who would lead me in. Not that I needed guidance after a while. Thinking my way through the maze to get to Beau had become part of the ritual I used to calm myself. Even now, I remember every step and every turn: the straight walk back through a quiet marble corridor, the right turn and transit across an intersection of two hallways, then the left into the elevator, and the ride to the second floor. I'd exit the elevator and make a hard left, then stop at the nurses' station to greet the team on duty and thank them for all they were doing. I tried not to dwell on the sights to the left of the station, where the rooms were full of patients who were not going to make it. That was not going to be my son, I'd tell myself as I headed to the right, toward Beau's room at the corner. And just before I got to his room I would begin to psych myself up. Smile, I'd say to myself. Smile. Smile. Smile. How many times Beau had said to me, "Don't look sad, Dad. You can't let anybody see you sad because it will make them feel bad. And I don't want anybody feeling sorry for me." You gotta make the final turn with a smile on your face, I'd

240

think. And then I'd make that turn and see either Hallie or Hunter or Jill or Ashley there, at the bedside, holding Beau's hand. "Hi, honey," I would say with all the cheer I could muster. "I'm here."

I came in one night anxious to tell Beau about the scene at the White House earlier in the day. "Honey," I said as I sat down by his bed, "guess who was at the office today?" Beau's eyes were closed, but I could tell he heard me. "Elton John was there," I said. "You remember when I used to drive you and Hunt to school? That song we would all sing together, the three of us, as loud as we could? 'Crocodile Rock.' " The boys were four and five when that song was big, when it was just the three of us. After Neilia died, but before I met Jill. I started singing the lyrics to Beau, quietly, so just the two of us could hear it. The words came back like it was yesterday, but after the first few lines I started to get emotional and wasn't sure if I could go on. Beau didn't open his eyes, but I could see through my own tears that he was smiling. So I gathered myself and kept at it, for as much of the song as I could remember.

The doctors were mulling the latest scan on the morning of May 15 and trying to find a way to relieve the constant pressure on Beau's brain, while I was trapped in the patient waiting room, which the White House communications team had converted into a private space where I could make secure calls. There was a new crisis in Iraq that day, and it needed my attention. Although I knew it was my responsibility, I felt for the first time a sense of resentment that I had to divert focus to anything other than Beau, even for just half an hour. My son was in one room in extremis and I was sitting in another, forced to deal with a problem sixty-two hundred miles away. The previous night, ISIL had blown into the city of Ramadi, west of Baghdad, under the cover of a blinding sandstorm. The first ISIL wave to hit the capital of Anbar Province was a convoy of armored vehicles. Many looked like something out of a *Mad Max* movie, appearing like a demonic vision through the wall of sand, led by giant steel plows welded onto the front. They were rolling bombs, loaded with explosives, with suicide drivers at the steering wheels. ISIL had reportedly massacred at least a dozen families and fifty policemen and tribal fighters in the early assault. The jihadists had already taken control of the main government buildings in Ramadi. The chairman of the provincial council was accusing Abadi of taking his eye off Ramadi and failing to live up to his promise to fund, train, and equip local Sunni tribal fighters.

When Abadi got on the phone with me that morning, ISIL was still on the attack — and gaining ground. The progovernment forces in the city did not have the where-withal to hold their defensive positions. Abadi said his soldiers simply lacked the firepower to push back the enormous armored truck bombs. He asked for antitank rockets so his men could knock the things out before they were on top of them, and he asked for more air strikes. I told him the antitank rockets were already in the pipeline, but we would send more and expedite delivery. I reassured him that the president and I were still behind him, but he needed to do a better job of getting money out of the banks and U.S. weapons out of the warehouses in Baghdad and into the hands of desperate Sunni tribal fighters near Ramadi. His security forces, all over the country, had to prove they could reclaim territory and then hold it. Taking back Ramadi, which was in the Sunni heartland of Iraq, would be an even bigger test than Tikrit. But we would help.

Abadi went on live television a few hours

later and told the Iraqi people that their military forces would stand and defend Ramadi from ISIL. He was sending reinforcements. "The next hours," he said, "will unfold with victory in Anbar." Less than forty-eight hours later, ISIL had taken over the entire city. They surrounded the Iraqi command center and pummeled it with waves of suicide bombers, slaughtering people trapped inside. At least five hundred Iraqi soldiers and local policemen fled Ramadi toward the safety of Baghdad, just sixty miles away. They left behind another enormous supply of valuable equipment and weapons for ISIL to take.

"All security forces and tribal leaders have either retreated or been killed in battle," lamented one Sunni tribal leader in Ramadi. "It is a big loss." The fall of Ramadi "represented the biggest victory so far this year for the Islamic State," the *New York Times* opined in its news coverage. "The defeat also laid bare the failed strategy of the Iraqi government."

The president convened a meeting of the National Security Council on May 19, and the focus was Ramadi. The debate among the principals was pretty hot. The most pessimistic view was that our strategy was in serious jeopardy because the Iraqi troops lacked real backbone. We could provide the Iraqis with military training, equipment, and weapons, and we could carry out air strikes, but we could not give Iraqi soldiers the courage to go out, take territory from ISIL, and hold it. This had been an ongoing concern of the president's from the beginning of the campaign against ISIL in Iraq. The project had been full of risk from the jump, and the president never received enough solid information to be sure-footed in his decision-making. A year earlier he had been wary of becoming too involved. He felt like we had our fingers in a dam, with no adequate measure of the power of the force on the other side. Could we contain ISIL? Could we control the war? Could we control the aftermath? The president was willing to put together a coalition to assist, but it was unlikely to succeed, he believed, without a legitimate Iraqi fighting force as a real partner. And, while Kurdish Peshmerga and Iranian-backed militias had reclaimed some terrain in the areas they coveted, there was very little evidence before May 2015 that Iraq's security forces were willing and able to reclaim and hold core Sunni territory.

But there was one big difference now; the president did have a little bit of hope to hold on to. Abadi had defeated ISIL in Tikrit just six weeks earlier, and he had done it with a non-sectarian force. When the prime minister had come to Washington two weeks after the victory in Tikrit, at my urging, for a long sit-down with the president, I think Barack saw in Abadi what I had seen. He was a partner worth backing.

The plan presented to President Obama by his key advisers on May 19, two days after the fall of Ramadi, made for a tough decision. We needed to get the Sunni tribal forces into the fight, our State and Defense Department colleagues emphasized. That required sending a few hundred special operations forces and advisers to Taqaddum air base, within fifteen miles of Ramadi, to help mobilize, train, and arm nearby Sunni tribes, and work with the Iraqi Army and Abadi's elite troops to coordinate the counteroffensive on Ramadi. My counsel was to give Abadi the help needed to reclaim the momentum from ISIL.

I got the sense that the president saw the logic of the strategy and was already inclined to pursue it, but he was worried about our ability to protect a few hundred Americans on the ground, operating out of an isolated air base in close proximity to Iranian-backed groups, at the edge of ISIL-controlled Anbar. "Joe," the president would say to me in private, "what happens if they go in and capture twenty of our guys and behead them? What the hell are we gonna do then?" He did not want our military dragged back into Iraq in a big way. And even if the counteroffensive on Ramadi did succeed, then what? Was there any guarantee the Iraqis could hold and govern the city once it was liberated? This was no easy call. But President Obama agreed to take it under advisement.

Something good was finally happening with Beau. The day Ramadi fell, he got out of bed for something approaching physical therapy. He was able to stand upright, with some help from the nurses, for five minutes. "Good day," Doc O'Connor recorded. Natalie and Hunter came by the day after to see their dad. Two days later a surgeon did a procedure that finally appeared to relieve the worst of the pressure in Beau's skull. He was becoming increasingly alert all the time. Doc told me he noticed Beau moving his upper arm on his long-paralyzed right side, and then his right thigh. The next day he was strong enough to sit up in a motorized wheelchair for a spin around the nurses' station. He was clearly aware again of what was happening, nodding his head in response to questions and giving fist bumps. Hallie got permission to take him for a ride outside, where he could feel the sun on his face for the first time in two and a half weeks. Seven weeks after the live virus injection, it looked like Beau had finally started to climb out of the dark hole.

Barack invited me to play golf that Saturday. He was worried about me, he explained, and hoped to distract me for a few hours. Jill encouraged me to go; it seemed, after all, like things were going to get better for Beau. The worst part is, I can't even remember whether or not I went.

A week after the fall of Ramadi, Secretary of Defense Ash Carter went on CNN and called out the men in the Iraqi military. "What apparently happened was that the Iraqi forces just showed no will to fight," Carter said in an interview that aired Sunday, May 24, on *State of the Union.* "They were not outnumbered. In fact, they vastly outnumbered the opposing force. And yet they failed to fight." This reflected the understandable skepticism some in our administration had about Iraq's willingness to take on ISIL. But I wish he hadn't said it.

When my team briefed me for my scheduled call with Prime Minister Abadi the next morning, Memorial Day, there was no surprise. Ambassador Jones and Deputy Special Envoy McGurk had been in touch with Iraqi officials, who all told them that Abadi was stung by Carter's statement and worried that Iraq was about to be abandoned. It wasn't hard to imagine what Abadi was feeling just then. When he told reporters, "It makes my heart bleed because we lost Ramadi," I knew his words were sincere. The briefers were all in agreement with me that my main task on the call that morning was to reinforce my belief in Abadi. He was under enormous pressure, and I wanted to make sure he heard me when I said we were still with him. I knew how tough Ramadi was, having been in the area in 2006 when the forerunner of ISIL, al-Qaeda in Iraq, controlled the city. Thousands of U.S. soldiers and marines, the most capable warriors in the world, fought like hell for four months to win back the city. Seventy-five U.S. service members and uncounted numbers of Iraqis were killed in that fight. I also knew, having watched Beau, the kind of sheer guts required to wage an uphill and scary battle against a vicious and remorseless foe. Knew how important it was to have real support.

Abadi was gracious on the call that morning. I didn't spend any time reminding him what we needed from him. He knew all that. I simply told him I recognized and appreciated the incredible sacrifices of Iraqi soldiers. I assured him the weapons and equipment we had promised were still in the pipeline. More important, I assured him that, despite Secretary Carter's statement, our administration had not lost faith in him. We remained committed to helping him turn the tide, because we still believed he could. I told him, as I had before, that he was a real leader, a man of both political and physical courage.

There was only one other small public event on my Memorial Day schedule before I could head over to Walter Reed to spend the holiday with Beau. I was anxious to see him, in part to see if there was more improvement and in part because I could not get out of my head the image of the dream I had the night before. Beau had appeared to me, completely cured, his old self again. The image was so vivid and felt so real. Beau was off in the distance, finishing one of his regular runs through the grounds of the Tatnall School, skirting the lake behind our house. I was trying desperately to find Jill or someone in the family, to share the amazing news. "I saw Beau running!" I wanted to shout. "I saw Beau running!"

Chapter Nine:
You Have to Tell Them
the Truth

When I got to Walter Reed on Memorial Day afternoon, Beau looked better to me than I'd seen him in weeks. He seemed to be more aware and responsive by the hour. The doctors thought maybe they finally had a handle on the chief problem: the pressure caused by the buildup of the cerebral spinal fluid in the left lateral ventricle of his brain. The ventricles of the brain produce, reabsorb, and drain cerebral spinal fluid in order to keep it in proper balance, but Beau's system wasn't draining properly. Doc O'Connor suggested to me that it might be a buildup of dead cancer cells that had sloughed and clogged the draining channel, like leaves in a gutter. The neurosurgeons at Reed had done a procedure a few days earlier that finally seemed to open up the pathway. Beau's left ventricle appeared to be clearing and shrinking. And there had been no evidence of cancer cells in the drained fluid. Medical researchers on the floor were really paying attention to Beau's progress now and were genuinely excited that they might be seeing the first success of its kind in the treatment of glioblastoma — this new combination of the live virus and anti-PD-1 antibody.

Keeping the fluid levels in Beau's ventricular system in balance and lowering the pressure on his brain was crucial to giving him relief from pain, and moments of clarity. And it was crucial to giving us hope. This was life or death now, and emotions were running high. Hallie, Jill, Ashley, and I all knew how critical it was to keep the cerebral spinal fluid perfectly balanced, and we were watching it almost hour by hour, vacillating between hope and despair. We also knew that because of the experimental nature of the live virus/anti-PD-1 treatment, it was important that Al Yung and Fred Lang be able to oversee the calibration. So the doctors at Reed were draining Beau's ventricular system every day and doing new scans to send down to M. D. Anderson. But the obstacles to communicating data between medical professionals in different hospitals persisted. As at Jefferson, the technicians at Walter Reed were unable to quickly and seamlessly transfer the scans to

M. D. Anderson. So Howard and Hunt had to once again find a way to take video or photographs of the scans with their personal iPhones or iPads and transmit them to Dr. Yung and Dr. Lang. There were times when I found them cursing this heartless system, because especially now, when Beau was really suffering, the loss of a day, an hour, even a minute, was real anguish for everyone in the family. My God, I thought to myself, there had to be a better way. I had to be able to do something about this.

And yet, in spite of this vexing reality, we were still seeing evidence that Beau might be about to turn the corner.

Jill and I were able to take Beau outside in his wheelchair that afternoon and the next evening, too, for a full half hour. The weather was mild for late May; it was eighty degrees in the twilight, with a slight cooling breeze. I knew Beau had to be in pain; I could see it in his eyes. But he seemed better. He occasionally nodded or smiled, or gave a thumbs-up. The sunset was just starting to color the clouds and I found myself remembering Beau as a little boy, sitting out on the balcony off my bedroom, looking out over the trees, watching the sunset. "Lookit, Daddy," he would say as the sun dropped below the tree line. "It's disappearing."

I was mildly upbeat when I headed out to make a speech early the next afternoon at the Brookings Institution, because Beau seemed to be improving. The subject of my talk that day was Ukraine, which was in trouble. Putin had kept constant pressure on Russia's neighbor country in the three months since the second Minsk agreement. He was still working hard to destabilize the Ukrainian economy and its government, and he had not pulled back his heavy artillery or his troops. In fact, we knew he had deployed as many as ten full battalions, along with air defense systems, near the border in the Rostov area alone. Two regular Russian soldiers had been wounded and captured in fighting *inside* Ukraine ten days earlier. The Russian-backed separatists — with Russian soldiers alongside them — had continued making sporadic but deadly attacks. And they gave no signs of backing away. At a meeting two weeks earlier, Putin had brushed aside Secretary of State John Kerry's reminder that the Russians needed to stop training and equipping separatist forces in Ukraine and that they needed to remove their troops from the border.

Ukraine's president, Petro Poroshenko,

was doing his best to keep his soldiers on the front lines from responding to provocations from the separatists and their Russian sponsors on the ground, but the cease-fire never really held. And yet, in the face of Putin's aggressive campaign to split Ukraine, Poroshenko was managing to hold his government together and move it toward greater transparency. I had been on the phone with either Poroshenko or his uneasy governing partner, Arseniy Yatsenyuk, or both, almost every week for the past three months, encouraging them to put patriotism above personal ambition. Working together, President Poroshenko and Prime Minister Yatsenyuk had taken the first steps toward important political reforms; the government had already established a national anticorruption bureau and Poroshenko had appointed its first head. We were doing what we could to help. We had, along with our European allies, widened the economic sanctions against Russia, and we had provided the Ukrainians another seventy-five million dollars' worth of nonlethal military equipment: armored personnel carriers, communications equipment, surveillance drones, and more countermortar radars. But in the last week in May, Putin had still not called off his dogs at Ukraine's border.

He remained in flagrant violation of the agreement he had signed.

News reports on the day of my speech at Brookings suggested that Putin was about to go a step further, putting the resolve of NATO, the EU, and the U.S. to a serious test. A Reuters correspondent had just returned from a Russian military encampment thirty miles from Ukraine, where he had witnessed the arrival of four separate trainloads of military equipment and troops. "The weapons being delivered there included Uragan multiple rocket launchers, tanks and self-propelled howitzers," the story read. "The amount of military hardware at the base was about three times greater than in March this year, when Reuters journalists were previously in the area."

The other ominous bit of news was that Putin was about to sign a decree banning the reporting of Russian deaths during "special operations" in peacetime — as it had long been banned in wartime. Putin wanted to bury any evidence of battle deaths in Ukraine, because two-thirds of the Russian population opposed the idea of sacrificing Russian soldiers to grab back pieces of Ukraine. "Some watchers can see only one plausible reason for the change," noted the *Washington Post.* "Russia is gearing up for another military push into Ukraine."

I was not going to pull any punches in this speech, because I knew everybody in the U.S. and in Europe would be paying attention. We had to extend the punishing sanctions on the Russian aggressors. We had to have a real debate about arming Ukrainians with weapons they could use to defend themselves. But more than that, it was time to call out Putin as a bully and to remind everybody that the West stood up to bullies. "We've reached another moment in the history of the transatlantic relationship that calls out for leadership, the kind our parents' and grandparents' generations delivered," I reminded the group at Brookings that day, and the world. "I think it's that basic. I think it's similar. I believe the terrain, though, is fundamentally in our favor. Not because of the inevitability of any kind of trajectory toward unification or integration or democratic freedoms. Every generation has its demagogues and revisionists, and transitions are full of peril that provides them with many, many opportunities.

"What makes me optimistic is that President Putin's vision has very little to offer the people of Europe — or, for that matter, the people of Russia — other than myths and illusions, the false promise of returning to a past that, when examined, was not too good a past to begin with. A sleight of hand that presents the bullying of civil societies, dissidents, and gays as substitutes for strong leadership and functioning institutions. The propaganda that conflates aggression with strength."

That evening when I got back to Walter Reed, Beau still appeared to be improving.

He had a bad night on Wednesday, and by the next afternoon, Thursday, he was barely responsive. No nods. No fist bumps. No thumbs-ups. We all prayed it was just another temporary setback, and Beau would come out of it — with a little extra ground to gain back. Somebody from the medical staff came into Beau's room to arrange a meeting for the next morning, when the doctors would give the family their assessment of Beau's condition and his prognosis. There would be new scans to look at by then. I thought the images would probably show more buildup of the cerebral spinal fluid. Once they drained it, Beau would be back in the game.

The whole family was gathered at ten o'clock Friday morning in a long, narrow conference room. The doctors from Walter Reed sat on one side of the table and the family on the other. There was a speaker-phone in the center, so the team from M. D. Anderson could weigh in also. The doctors, including Doc O'Connor and Ashley's husband, Howard, had clearly been talking among themselves, and they seemed fairly united in their message. The physicians did not like what they saw. The scans looked far worse than they had just two days earlier. But the doctors couldn't be sure if it was the virus at work or the tumor.

I was still looking for a way through it, out to the other side, with Beau alive. And I think the rest of the family felt the same way. After about forty-five minutes, one of the doctors from Walter Reed finally said it might be worth waiting for another twenty-four or forty-eight hours, and see what happens. We all filed out of the conference room and walked back down the hall toward Beau's room feeling hopeful, holding on to the idea that he might pull out of this again. But then we heard Howard's voice behind us. "You've got to come back," he said, as he steered us again to the conference room. "You have to tell them the truth," Howard said to the doctors still assembled. What was happening in Beau's brain was no longer reversible, the doctors said. There was no saving Beau. "He will not recover."

These were the most devastating four words I have ever heard in my life. "He will not recover." But goddammit, I still wanted to believe — maybe — maybe something will happen.

Hallie asked Howard if she should bring the kids down on Monday, and he told her, no, Hallie, you have to bring the kids here now. Hallie's parents drove Natalie and Hunter down from Wilmington that evening. They came down the hallways of the hospital smiling, as if it were just another visit. Hallie had her children by the hand, walking them past the nurses' station, toward Beau's room. The Secret Service agents, many of whom had been with our family for more than six years, bowed their heads and stared at the marble floor, or turned away, so nobody would see them weeping as Natalie and Hunter went by.

Nobody left the hospital that night. Hunter's wife and daughters came to be with us. My sister Val, her husband Jack, my brother Jim and his wife Sarah were there with us. My niece Missy, who had grown up with Beau, came to be with us, too. And we waited, all of us, together. Hunter and Howard left the floor briefly, just after seven

261

o'clock that night, to pick up food for the family. And not long after they walked out, Beau's breathing became labored, and then extremely shallow, and then appeared to stop. There was no heartbeat registering on the monitor. Hunt and Howard raced back, and when they arrived they found the rest of us gathered around Beau. Hunt walked over, bent down to kiss him, and placed his hand over his brother's heart. Howard looked at the monitor. "Look," he said. Beau's heart was beating again.

It didn't last long.

May 30. 7:51 p.m. It happened, I recorded in my diary. *My God, my boy. My beautiful boy.*

Jill and I arrived home in Delaware on Air Force Two at about eight o'clock on Sunday night, almost exactly twenty-four hours after Beau passed. General Frank Vavala, the commander of the Delaware National Guard, in which Beau had served, was waiting to greet us on the tarmac, his wife by his side. By the time we reached them, the general and his wife were both in tears, and they could not stop crying. "We loved Beau," he said. Jill and I were on the tarmac for almost five minutes trying to console them, and when we finally got in our car and pulled away I saw the general standing there, ramrod straight, saluting. And sobbing.

Jill wanted to go to our dock as soon as we got home, so we took Champ down the slope of the hill and walked out over the edge of the lake. This was one of the longest days of the year, so there was still light in the sky when we sat down, and Jill spotted a white egret at the far edge of the water. She said it made her feel more connected to Beau, being here at a place he loved so deeply. She told me that at one point, in the final hours, she had leaned in and whispered to him, "Go to a happy place, Beau. Go to the dock, with Hunter." We watched the egret for twenty minutes, until it finally took flight. The two of us sat in silence as the egret circled overhead repeatedly, slowly gaining altitude, until it finally headed away to the south, beneath the clouds, and gradually disappeared from sight. "It's a sign from God," Jill said. "Beau being at the lake one last time, and heading for heaven."

Jill went in to bed not long after and I ended up alone in the sitting room off our bedroom, which had just been wallpapered. The room was still in disarray from the job; the furniture was moved aside and books and mementos were shoved into the middle of the floor in open boxes or piles. I asked a couple of Secret Service agents to help me move Jill's desk and my credenza back into place, but that didn't take long. I needed something to do to keep my mind occupied until I could sleep, so I started emptying some of the boxes and replacing the books — methodically, by subject matter — on the shelves. The last box I grabbed held some pages from scrapbooks and some old family photos. The photograph on top of the pile fluttered out, so I bent down to pick it up; it was a four-by-six color photo of Beau. He was probably eight or nine, in sneakers and shorts, wearing a baseball cap and a jacket, walking through the hedgerows at the Station, the house I bought soon after Neilia died. The boys and Ashley had grown up there. In the photo, Beau was walking away from me, looking over his shoulder, smiling and waving. I was suddenly overwhelmed. I had not seen that photo in at least three decades, but it was the age I always pictured him in my mind. Always smiling at me, with that look of reassurance.

My God, it struck me in that moment, I miss him so terribly — already. Beau could always chase my fears away. He saved my life, along with Hunter, forty years ago, after Neilia and Naomi died in the car accident, and now what was I supposed to do? I had looked to Beau, as I looked to Hunt, from the time he was a child, as a source of confidence and courage. "It's going to be okay, Daddy," he would say. "I'm not going away." How foolish it sounds, I thought, that a grown man, an accomplished man, who spent his whole life trying to communicate courage and fortitude, had to look to his own sons to buck him up. "Look at me, Dad," I could almost hear Beau say. "Remember. Remember. Home base."

I have been a public man for almost fifty years, which means my children and grandchildren have been part of a public family their entire lives. They knew without my ever saying it that the way we conducted ourselves over the next week, the way we said good-bye to Beau, mattered enormously. He, too, was a public man — a loved and respected figure in Delaware — so he would have to be celebrated, and mourned, in public. There was a schedule already taking shape. On Thursday, we would all be driving down to the state capital of Dover, with the body in a flag-draped coffin; Beau would lie in honor during a four-hour ceremony in Legislative Hall. Then we would fly back to Washington that evening for Maisy Biden's eighth-grade graduation. Friday morning was Beau's daughter Natalie's fourth-grade graduation in Wilmington, then the private family mass at our home parish, St. Joseph's on the Brandywine, followed by a public wake at St. Anthony's, in the heart of Wilmington. Saturday was the memorial service, the Mass of Christian Burial, also at St. Anthony's, followed by the interment in our family plot at St. Joseph's. All through the planning, I was mindful of concentric circles of obligation — obligations to Beau, to his wife and children, to my wife and my other children, to my other grandchildren, to my brothers and sister, to my extended family, to my friends, but also to everyone who came to the wakes or the funeral, or watched the proceedings on television, some of which were to be broadcast live across the country. I believed it was my public duty to demonstrate to those millions of people facing the same awful reality that it was possible to absorb real loss and make it through. My family and I had an obligation to show perseverance and grace.

Hallie and my sister Val and Hunter and I planned out almost every step of the days to come. We made charts and diagrams of where we would walk and sit and stand. But as we bent to the task, I noticed that Hunter, determined to honor Beau's wishes, took the lead. He knew how his brother would want to be remembered — as a husband, a father, a public man who meant to serve *all,* and a soldier — and he was determined to infuse the proceedings with the vital red blood of Beau's life. He called Protestant ministers, a Jewish rabbi, and a Muslim cleric and invited them to be on the altar along with the Roman Catholic cardinal and priests; he made sure Beau's National Guard brigade had a place in the ceremony and arranged for a horse-drawn hearse to carry Beau's casket through the streets of Wilmington, which would be lined with a military honor guard and the police Beau had led as attorney general. Hunt selected an African American choral group to bring joyful music to the service and bagpipers to add the mournful, plaintive wail of Irishness.

The final touch was a special gift from Hallie to the children. They had been riding in a car one afternoon when a Coldplay song came on the radio. "That's Daddy's favorite," nine-year-old Hunter said. Hunter had taken possession of his father's iPod by then, and Hallie noticed that he kept playing " 'Til Kingdom Come" over and over.

So Hallie called Beth Buccini, whose husband Robbie was Beau's best friend, and who had a way to get a message to Coldplay's lead singer, Chris Martin. Martin agreed to fly in from London to perform the song at the mass, and Robbie Buccini generously agreed to pick up the tab for all of his travel expenses.

Barack had offered to do the main eulogy for Beau — an offer we accepted. And Beau's overall commander in Iraq, General Ray Odierno, also agreed to speak. The general, now chief of staff of the U.S. Army, had called two days after Beau died to ask if he and his wife could attend the funeral. "I really expected Beau would be leading our country one day," he said to me. I thought it best that Ashley and Hunter speak for the family, that they should be the ones to stand up and eulogize their brother. And they agreed. But despite the meticulous planning, when we all stepped out of our home together for the first public event, nobody in the family was under the illusion that this would be easy.

When it was all finally behind us, Saturday night, June 6, I found myself sitting alone in my library. Beau had been gone for exactly a week, but I could still feel his presence. *It doesn't seem real yet,* I wrote in my diary that night. *I was so intent on this being dignified and powerful for Beau's memory, I willed myself to not focus on the enormity, on the black hole in my chest, pulling me in. By focusing on Hunt and Ash I've been able to pretend Beau is still with me. Even today, with the exception of [the rendition of] the song "Bring Him Home" I put Beau in the middle of everything, as if he and I were pulling all of this together.*

Sitting there, reflecting on the past three days, I had flashes of incredible pride in my son and my family; a sense of accomplishment threaded through my wall of grief. Beau "cared deeply for his fellow human beings and always treated everyone with dignity and respect," General Odierno had said in his funeral speech. "He had a natural charisma that few people possess. People willingly wanted to follow him, completely trusted his judgment, and believed in him." I was still moved by the thought of Barack's willingness to let go and show the extraordinary depth of his emotion in his eulogy for Beau. We had been through a lot together, but I felt closer to the president that day in St. Anthony's, and more appreciative of his friendship, than ever before. "Michelle and I and Sasha and Malia, we've become part of the Biden clan, we're honorary members now," he said. "And the Biden family rule applies: We're always here for you. We always will be. My word as a Biden."

When Ashley and Hunt ascended to the altar there was an absolute hush in the congregation. Everyone in the audience knew the depth of the loss each of them felt, and I knew from my own experience how difficult it is to eulogize someone you adore. They were in such pain, and summoning composure required remarkable courage. I have never been prouder of my son and daughter. When they spoke of their brother, there was something almost holy about it — as if they were willing their own Trinity to abide. "It's impossible to talk about Beau without talking about Hunter," Ashley told the gathering, in a speech she insisted on writing herself. "Hunter was the wind beneath Beau's wings. Hunt gave him the courage and the confidence to fly. . . . There wasn't one decision where Hunter wasn't consulted first, not one day that passed where they didn't speak, and not one road traveled where they weren't each other's copilots. Hunter was Beau's confidant. His home.

"When I was born, I was welcomed with open arms and held tightly by both Beau-y and Hunt-y, as I adoringly called them my whole life. The boys named me. I was theirs and I felt as though they were mine."

Hunter stood by Ashley as she spoke, and when he stepped up to the microphone, Ashley remained to stand by her brother while he did the thank-yous on behalf of the entire family. "The first memory I have is of lying in a hospital bed next to my brother," Hunter began, recounting the days they were together in the hospital, recovering from the car accident that had taken the lives of their mother and sister. "I was almost three years old. I remember my brother, who was one year and one day older than me, holding my hand, staring into my eyes, saying, 'I love you, I love you, I love you,' over and over and over again. And in the forty-two years since, he never stopped holding my hand, he never stopped telling me just how much he loves me. But mine wasn't the only hand Beau held. Beau's was the hand everyone reached for in their time of need. Beau's was the hand that was reaching for yours before you even had to ask." Hunter spoke for almost twenty-five minutes, about Beau's journey through life and all the people he touched. He captured the essence of his brother, without a single false note. Hunter concluded, "He held so many hands. Survivors of abuse, parents of his fallen brothers and sisters in uniform, victims of violent crime in his beloved city of Wilmington. That's my brother's story; there are thousands of people telling those stories right now. Telling the same story, about when Beau Biden held their hand. My only claim on my brother is that he held my hand first. . . .

"And as it began, so did it end. His family surrounded him, everyone holding on to him, each of us desperately holding him. Each of us saying, 'I love you, I love you, I love you.' And I held his hand, and he took his last breath, and I know that I was loved. And I know that his hand will never leave mine."

I am blessed with a magnificent family. I remember thinking how lucky we were, just to be able to physically hold on to one another through the three days of public ceremonies. When one of us flagged or started to lose composure, there was always somebody there for support. "C'mon, Dad," I heard Hunt say when he noticed me looking up to the ceiling and saw my shoulders start to shake. It is a blessing to be able to share the feeling of enveloping grief, to have people you love nearby to absorb some of

272

the worst pain. But I have come to understand that nobody can really take away all the pain, no matter how close. There are times when each of us must bear the burden of loss alone, and in his or her own way. The people who really understand that are the people carrying those burdens, too. And they are another real source of solace. Of all the calls and visits in that difficult week, all the heartfelt condolences and the well-wishes from the thousands of people who filed through the receiving lines, one stood out. It happened at the public wake, at St. Anthony's in Wilmington, on the day before the funeral mass. I was there with Jill and the rest of the family for hours, standing by Beau's casket, as thousands of friends, acquaintances, and supporters filed by. People came from all over the country — including the nurses from Walter Reed and Jefferson hospitals — but most were from Delaware. Our home state is a small place, and I had been there for many years, so I recognized most of the mourners by face, if not by name. But at one point, I looked up and saw in the line, approaching me, Wei Tang Liu, the father of the Chinese American police officer who had been killed on duty in New York City five months earlier. He and his wife had made the three-hour drive from their home in Brooklyn to Wilmington, then stood for hours in a line of people that snaked for blocks down the sidewalk, into the church, and right up to Beau's coffin.

Wei Tang Liu did not try to speak, and neither did I. He still didn't have the English, and I still didn't have the Cantonese. He just walked up and gave me a hug. It meant so much to me to be in the embrace of somebody who understood. He held on to me, silently, and wouldn't let go. This was not, as it had been the last time we met, for him. This was for me. "Thank you" was all I could say. "Thank you. Thank you. Thank you."

CHAPTER TEN:
CAN YOU STAY?

I had been here before and knew what to expect. Shock creates an initial numbness that wears away. The pain comes then, and it sharpens. The hurt is a physical presence, and it never leaves you. As when I lost Neilia and Naomi forty-three years earlier, it felt like there was a tiny dark hole in the middle of my chest, and I knew if I dwelled on its presence, it would grow until it threatened to suck my entire being down into it. There were times when it seemed easier to just disappear into that void, into the merciful *absence* of pain. I remember not being able to take a long, deep breath for months. My religious faith provided some refuge from the pain. I've always found comfort in the ritual associated with my Catholicism. I find the rosary soothing. It's almost like my meditation. And mass is a place I go to be by myself, even in the middle of the crowd. I always feel alone, just me and God. When I pray, I find myself not only praying to God, but praying to Neilia and to my mom to intercede with God for me. It's a way of reminding myself that they are still a part of me, still inside me. And in the first hours after we lost Beau, I began to talk to him, too. It was my way to remind myself that he was still here with me, too.

Ashley captured the truth of it, and the need of it, at the end of her eulogy. "You will be with us for every decision we make in moments of sadness and struggle, and celebration and joy," she said of Beau, and I knew she was speaking directly to me and the rest of our family. "We will see you everywhere we go, in the beauty of nature, in a smile from strangers, and in your beautiful children, who we will take care of like you took care of all of us. You were etched in every fiber of our being. You are the bone of our bones, the flesh of our flesh, and blood of our blood. You are ever present in our lives, today, tomorrow, and forever."

Whenever I thought of those words, the thought crossed my mind: as long as I have Hunt, I have Beau. They were inseparable in life and they are inseparable in death. Even now, Beau was present for me. He was more than present. He was the voice in my head. The words I kept replaying, over and over, were his. Beau and Hallie had invited us over to dinner one evening the previous fall when the physical effects of the cancer were becoming undeniable. Jill had arrived on a train from Wilmington, having finished a day of teaching, and came straight to the house in her work clothes. After we were finished eating she said she wanted to go home and change into something more comfortable. "Can you stay, Dad?" Beau asked me. "Hallie and I want to talk to you."

He asked Hallie to take Natalie and Hunter upstairs, and waited for her to return. The two of them sat across from me at their long narrow table. "Dad, look," he said. "I know no one in the whole world loves me as much as you do. I know that.

"But Dad, look at me. Look at me. I'm going to be okay no matter what happens. I'm going to be okay, Dad. I promise you." I was jolted by the realization that my son was beginning to make peace with his own death. Then he leaned across the table and put his hand on my arm. "But you've got to promise me, Dad, that no matter what happens, you're going to be all right. Give me your word, Dad, that you're going to be all right. Promise me, Dad."

"I'm going to be okay, Beau," I said, but that wasn't enough for him.

"No, Dad," he said. "Give me your word as a Biden. Give me your word, Dad. Promise me, Dad."

I promised.

Nobody at the White House expected me to be back at work right away. President Obama and his closest aides went out of the way to signal to me in private and in public that they would continue to give me whatever space and time I needed to heal. "It doesn't end when the service ends — and in a sense that's the beginning," the president's friend and close adviser Valerie Jarrett told a reporter. "He will be surrounded with love and support and given whatever he needs. It's a long grieving process, and I think part of friendship is understanding that, and being there for the long haul." I also had an incredible foreign policy team that had continued to do what needed to be done in my absence. My national security adviser, Colin Kahl, was overseeing everything, with particular focus on Iraq. Michael Carpenter was keeping the watch on Ukraine; Juan Gonzalez on the Northern Triangle. There were Victoria Nuland at the State Department and Charlie

Kupchan on the White House NSC staff handling Russia; Brett McGurk in Iraq, Syria, and Turkey; Jeffrey Prescott in the Far East; Amos Hochstein on energy policy around the world. I had incredible support, and they would have carried the ball for as long as I needed them to. But I could not sit home with my grief. I knew I had to be engaged.

I decided I would report for duty four days after Beau's service to let the president know I was ready to get back to work. I needed to be working, to be occupied. For my own sanity, I needed to keep busy. The president was just back from the G-7 summit in Germany, where he had pressed Chancellor Merkel and other European leaders to continue and even enlarge the economic sanctions against Russia until Putin lived up to the Minsk cease-fire agreement and backed off in Ukraine. I really appreciated how forcefully the president had staked out the ground. "Russia has essentially thumbed their nose at the commitments that they made," the president's chief spokesman announced. "Russia's failure to live up to those commitments is what leads to their increasing isolation and the increasing costs being imposed on their economy." Prime Minister Yatsenyuk was visiting

Washington that day, and I needed to be there to deliver the message that we were standing by the Ukrainian people and their government, but also to make sure he understood that he and Poroshenko needed to speed up anticorruption reforms if they wanted continued assistance.

Two days later I was scheduled to meet with the speaker of the Iraqi Council of Representatives, Salim al-Jabouri, the political leader of the Sunnis. The fall of Ramadi had put intense pressure on the Abadi government. But President Obama had strengthened his commitment to Jabouri and to Abadi. He had just authorized the risky deployment of U.S. military advisers to an air base within fifteen miles of Ramadi to help mobilize, train, and equip Sunni tribal fighters for the coming counterattack. So I wanted to make sure Jabouri heard from me the critical importance of Iraqi unity in the face of the continuing ISIL threat.

Five days after the Jabouri meeting, I was to receive Honduran president Juan Orlando Hernández in Washington to show him our administration remained serious about providing assistance if they remained serious about implementing the reforms we had agreed on in Guatemala City in early

March. I needed to get back up to speed on everything.

When I walked back into the office on Wednesday, June 10, it felt like Beau was watching and talking to me. "Dad, don't let them see your pain, Dad," he would say. "Get up. One foot in front of the other. Keep moving."

President Obama and I had lunch that first day, right before my meeting with Arseniy Yatsenyuk. The president had come to know me pretty well. He knew it would help me to stay deeply involved in our work, to keep my focus on something other than Beau. So he stuck to business that day, and we spent almost the entire lunch talking about our foreign policy goals. But when I reported to him what my team and I had been doing in Ukraine, Iraq, and the Northern Triangle, I think he was surprised at how engaged I was. The president asked me to think about what other specific assignments I wanted for our last eighteen months in office, what new challenges I wanted to tackle. I knew I wanted to finish what I had started in Ukraine, Iraq, and the Northern Triangle, but I wasn't sure exactly what the near future held for me. So I told him I would get back to him.

There were more than seventy thousand notes and letters of condolence waiting for me at the White House, along with what had to be close to a thousand statements from public officials, foreign dignitaries, and political commentators. Friends and colleagues who were closest to Beau were the most incisive, which meant their messages were both heartening and heartbreaking: *It was an honor to serve alongside him as he worked tirelessly to fight for the powerless and protect the most vulnerable, our children. . . . Add to that his spark, genuineness, earnestness, and unconditional love for public service. . . . One of the truest measures of the man is that he never lost a friend. That tells you everything about him. . . . He was honestly a great dad. He was the type of father who was present with his children. . . . Beau made every game. He knew every kid's name and rooted as hard for them as he did for his own son. . . . Family came first. Family was the beginning, middle, and end for him.* A friend of Beau's from grade school told a story about running into him a few years earlier, when Beau, Hallie, and the kids were living with Jill and me while they renovated their house. The friend wondered about the difficulty of living with his parents again. "Beau said how wonderful it was for the whole family to be living under the same roof," the friend explained. "Being together as family was the most important thing for him."

There were two letters that gave me real comfort in the first days after Beau's passing. One was from Evan Ryan, one of my former staff members. She sent me a note, quoting a poem. "I stood watching as the little ship sailed out to sea," it read. "The setting sun tinted his white sails with a golden light, and as he disappeared from sight a voice at my side whispered, 'He is gone.'" The disappearance did not mark an end, but another beginning, in a new and unknown place. "On the farther shore a little band of friends had gathered to watch and wait in happy expectation." I found myself imagining Neilia, and Beau's baby sister, Naomi, and my own mother and father standing on that far shore, ready to receive him. "Suddenly they caught sight of the tiny sail and, at the very moment when my companion had whispered, 'He is gone,' a glad shout went up in joyous welcome, 'Here he comes.'"

A personal letter from Teddy Kennedy's

widow, Vicki, struck me especially. Vicki had married into a singular family in American history. The Kennedys had enjoyed soaring accomplishment and suffered devastating tragedy. Their experience seemed to confirm my father's belief that fate was an inescapable part of life, but that every person, and every family, got a kind of zero balance in the good fortune–bad fortune equation on the ledger sheet. The bigger the highs, the deeper the troughs. My own life bore out his adage. The Kennedys were on a whole other level. Teddy's father, Joe Kennedy Sr., had been a spectacular success in almost every business he touched, and he had seen one of his sons become president of the United States. But he buried three of his four sons and a treasured daughter in his own lifetime. In her letter to me, Vicki Kennedy quoted from a letter Joe Sr. had written to a friend who had lost his own son, a letter she said Teddy used to pull out and read in the worst times of his own life. "When one of your loved ones goes out of your life, you think what he might have done with a few more years," Joe Sr. had written to his friend. "And you wonder what you are going to do with the rest of yours. Then one day, because there is a world to be lived in, you find yourself part of it, trying to accomplish something — something he did not have time enough to do. And perhaps that is the reason for it all. I hope so." I hope so, too.

I knew what Beau would have done with a few more years. He would have continued his fight against the abuse of power, especially the abuse of children. It was central to who he was, and Hunter, Hallie, Ashley, Jill, and I were determined to carry that effort forward in his honor. We set up the Beau Biden Foundation to continue his work. It gave us purpose. And we all needed purpose.

The president may have been a little taken aback at our lunch six days later. He asked me again what assignments I wanted for the remainder of our administration. I was noncommittal. "What are you going to do," he asked, "about running?" I explained that I had not entirely set aside the idea of running for the Democratic nomination in 2016. I hadn't decided yet, and I knew I wouldn't be in any position to make the decision for a while. And then I found myself saying, "Look, Mr. President, I understand if you've made an explicit commitment to Hillary and to Bill Clinton," but I assured Barack that if I did decide to run

I would engage Hillary on our policy differences only and not on questions of character or personality that might weaken her if she won the nomination. "I promise you," I said. And we left it at that.

The next day was the busiest I had had since my return — a full calendar. The daily intelligence briefing, followed by a meeting to prepare a speech I was giving at the State Department the next week about the necessity of increasing our economic engagement with China, followed by a briefing on Central America, followed by my meeting with President Hernández. And then I was flying home to Wilmington so Jill and I could spend our anniversary together. We were in no mood for celebration, but we did want to be together.

June 17. Good day in that I was busy and was able to have some relief, I wrote in my diary in Wilmington that night. *Still not believable to me that Beau is gone. I feel his presence as much as I did when he was in Iraq for a year. I know if I'm unable to compartmentalize I'll go nuts. I can hear him saying, "Now, Dad, I'm all right. It's all good. All good, Dad."*

Jill was downhearted that night. Summer was usually her favorite time of year, but there was no joy in it now. I wanted to be able to ease Jill's pain, but I understood there was only so much I could do. I was hoping, but not at all convinced, that our upcoming trip might help. We were just a week away from a family vacation to one of our favorite beach spots, in South Carolina, and everybody seemed apprehensive about the trip. It was going to be difficult for us to all be together for the first time, in a place Beau loved, without him. But I had made the case that in the aftermath of our loss it was even more important that we continue to do the things that had always meant so much to the family. That we could not let our traditions drift away. That Beau would have wanted us to make the trip. I knew from past experience that as hard as it would be, it was better to go through it than to avoid it. We needed real family time together. So we agreed to try the week at the beach on Kiawah Island. The family was going to fly down on Tuesday, June 23, and I would follow a few days later.

The lead-up to the trip and the trip itself ended up being even more of an emotional roller coaster than I had anticipated. On our anniversary night, six days before Jill was scheduled to leave, came word that nine innocent people had been killed at a black church in Charleston, South Carolina. Among the victims was the pastor of Emanuel AME Church, the Reverend Clementa Pinckney — a man I had come to know. Reverend Pinckney was a state senator making his mark in South Carolina politics, and I had spent time with him at political events in the past few years. He was just forty-one years old, younger even than Beau, with a wife and two daughters, ages eleven and six.

The killer was a twenty-one-year-old white supremacist who had walked into the church that evening, accepted an invitation to join the Wednesday night Bible study, sat for the last half hour of the meeting, and then viciously gunned down nine of the twelve people in the group. The oldest victim was eighty-seven years old, the youngest twenty-six. Among the assassin's professed goals was igniting a race war. Jill and I made a public statement that night, and I began making arrangements to call the families of the victims to offer our condolences. And then we began to steel ourselves for the added event on our schedule the following week. We would be making the trip from Kiawah to Charleston to attend the public memorial for Reverend Pinckney and other Emanuel victims, and to do what we could to bring some small measure of comfort to their families and friends.

I gave Jill a couple of small gifts the next night to try to lift her spirits, but it seemed to have the opposite effect. She said she didn't want dinner. She had a cup of soup and went up to bed at eight thirty, while it was still light outside. I was talking to Hunter when she went up. Hunt was trying hard to keep me moving forward to the next big goal. He knew Beau's wishes better than I did, but he also knew me.

"If God appeared to you tomorrow, Dad," he told me, "and said, 'The nomination is yours, but you have to decide now,' I know you would say no."

"In my heart," I told Hunter, "I honestly believe that if we run we have a really good chance of winning."

Hunter went on to remind me that our family, devastated or not, would grow closer and stronger under the pressure of a presidential campaign.

We both knew that the family had always been at its best when we had a clear purpose to unify around, especially when we were up against long odds. But the toll of losing Beau made this an entirely new circumstance. I just wasn't sure that I was emotionally ready and up to the task, which would be an enormous undertaking even in the best of circumstances.

We were in Kiawah at just after ten o'clock on the morning of June 26, preparing for the ride to the memorial service in Charleston, when the news broke. "A historic day here at the Supreme Court," came the report from CNN, from just outside the court. "You can probably hear gay rights advocates to my right cheering this decision, authored by Justice Kennedy, saying that the right to marriage is a fundamental right and gays and lesbians cannot be excluded from that right. In this broad ruling by Justice Kennedy, he says 'the right to marry is a fundamental right,' and same-sex couples may not be deprived of liberty, or that right to marriage. So again, ruling today that same-sex marriage is a nation-wide constitutional right. This is one of the greatest civil rights issues of our time and this is what gay rights advocates have been hoping for for decades."

The decision was 5–4. Justice Anthony Kennedy, who was sworn in during the final year of Ronald Reagan's presidency, was not only the swing vote but also the author of the majority opinion in the landmark decision. I took some real pride in the ruling, in part because I had been the Judiciary Committee chairman who had presided over Kennedy's confirmation hearings. Anthony Kennedy wasn't Reagan's first choice. He was only nominated after the confirmation hearings for Reagan's original pick, Robert Bork, had revealed Bork to be so narrow in his reading of the fundamental privacy rights afforded by the Constitution that the Senate had rejected him, 58–42. The no votes included six from Reagan's own party. I had worked hard in that hearing to be fair to Bork, who was a distinguished jurist and a remarkably intelligent man. But I also worked hard to show that Judge Bork's views and his record of jurisprudence were at odds with how most Americans viewed our Constitution. Judge Bork believed there were no individual rights in the Constitution that were not literally written into the document itself. The Constitution did not speak explicitly of the right to privacy, or the right to use contraception, or the right of women to be treated equally under the law, or the right to marry somebody of the same sex, so it required a legislature to grant those rights. Courts, in Bork's view, had to defer to the political process in all those matters. Majority rules.

I could tell from Anthony Kennedy's testimony in his nomination hearing that he would have a much more generous reading of the Constitution and a much more expansive view of individual rights and equality under the law, and history has shown that to be the case. His majority opinion in the 2015 gay marriage case was the high mark of his three decades on the court.

The fight for marriage equality was a long, slow battle that required incredible moral and physical courage on the part of really brave gay men and women. Just being public about who they were was an act of courage until not so long ago. Gays and lesbians who came out, stood up, and made their case for equal treatment and equal rights risked a hell of a lot. They demanded their rights in the face of flat-out hatred in a few quarters, which made them prey to physical and emotional abuse. I remember that during the awful scourge of AIDS, many in the conservative fundamentalist clergy and many right-wing officials cruelly claimed that the disease killing thousands of young gay men every year was a judgment from God. But the toughest obstacle gays and lesbians faced was probably not hatred; it was the ignorance of most of their fellow citizens. It took a long time for Americans to begin to understand the simple and obvious truth that gay men and women are overwhelmingly good, decent, honorable people who want and deserve the same rights as anyone else. I didn't fully grasp the pervasiveness of the difficulty they faced until one night in the 1990s. I was a senator then, and got on a train to go back to Wilmington after a Judiciary Committee hearing about gays in the military. One of the men servicing the snack bar of the Amtrak train, a guy I had known for years, had been watching the proceedings and was really demoralized by some of the talk he heard from the antigay crowd. "You know, Senator," he said to me, "I'm gay."

"No, I didn't know that," I said.

"I've got two sons, and one is also gay," he told me. "And you know what gets me about these guys? They think that this is a 'behavior.' They think we woke up one morning and said, 'Goddamn, wouldn't it be great to be gay? Wouldn't it be great to be gay? Goddamn, this will make life easier. Wouldn't it be wonderful. I think I'll be gay.'"

I also remember watching a Senate colleague struggle to comprehend the testimony of Jeffrey Levi, the executive director of the National Gay and Lesbian Task Force, who came to provide testimony at a Judiciary Committee hearing in 1986. Levi made one of the last appearances of the many representatives from outside groups who came in to offer statements at the tail end of the confirmation hearings for William Rehnquist's nomination to be chief justice.

By the time Levi began his statement, Strom Thurmond and I were the only two committee members left at the hearing — the only two there when the witness presented the statistic that about 10 percent of the American population is gay, which means something like thirty million Americans. Strom was genuinely stunned. I think the eighty-four-year-old senator, who had been in elective office since 1933, truly believed he had never known a gay person. "Joe," Strom said to me during Levi's statement, "is that *true*?" I quietly whispered to Strom that some experts did argue that up to 10 percent of the population is gay.

Strom turned to the young, well-spoken, conservatively dressed witness. "Are you sure that figure is correct?" he asked. Levi then cited the statistics developed a generation earlier by renowned sex researcher Alfred Kinsey. Strom had a hard time processing this fact and wandered down a line of questioning that was not intended to be mean-spirited, but was nonetheless wounding.

"Does your organization advocate any kind of treatment for gays and lesbians to see if they can change them and make them normal like other people?"

"Well, Senator, we consider ourselves to be quite normal, thank you. We just happen to be different from other people. And the beauty of American society is that, ultimately, we do accept all differences of behavior and viewpoint. . . . It is — all the responsible medical community no longer considers homosexuality to be an illness but rather something that is just a variation of standard behavior."

"You don't think gays and lesbians are subject to change, or you don't think they could —"

"No more so, Senator, than —"

"— you don't think they could be converted so they'd be like other people, in some way?"

"Well, we think we are like other people, with one small exception. And unfortunately, it's the rest of society that makes a big deal out of that exception."

"A small exception? It's a pretty big

exception, isn't it?"

"Unfortunately, society makes it a big exception."

Strom put his hand over his microphone and turned to me. "I think I should go," he said, "shouldn't I?"

Well, as of June 26, 2015, the law of the land would no longer make exceptions in recognizing marriage. "In forming a marital union, two people become something greater than once they were. As some of the petitioners in these cases demonstrate, marriage embodies a love that may endure even past death," Kennedy had written in the opinion he read aloud at the Supreme Court that morning. "Their hope is not to be condemned to live in loneliness, excluded from one of civilization's oldest institutions. They ask for equal dignity in the eyes of the law. The Constitution grants them that right."

I cannot claim to have risked much in advocating equality for the LGBT community. But I felt incredibly proud that day to have played some role in the gay marriage decision. I thought of Beau, who as attorney general of Delaware made a point of attending a same-sex wedding on July 1, 2013, the day marriage equality was implemented in our state. He had also filed a legal brief supporting marriage equality in a case before the Ninth Circuit back in the fall of 2013, when he was just finishing his first round of radiation and chemotherapy. A few months later he announced that Delaware would recognize same-sex marriages performed in Utah in the narrow window of time when it was legal there. "Marriage equality is the law in Delaware," he had said, "and I strongly believe that individuals outside our state borders should be equally free to choose whom to love and whom to spend their lives with."

I also thought of my dad that morning in Kiawah, and one of the greatest life lessons he taught me, when I was a teenager. We were at a traffic light in downtown Wilmington, and my dad and I caught a glimpse of two men on a nearby corner. They embraced, kissed each other, and then headed off separately to face their days — as I supposed thousands of husbands and wives all over the city did every morning. I just turned and looked at my dad for an explanation. "Joey, it's simple," my dad told me. "They love each other."

Barack spoke at the memorial service in Charleston later that afternoon, and he did it magnificently. I'm not sure I ever saw him make a better speech. I focused my own attention on physically embracing the victims' families I had already spoken to, to offer what comfort I could. And at the funeral, after meeting the families in person, I decided I wanted to go back to Charleston two days later for the regular Sunday services at Emanuel AME Church. I didn't want to draw attention to my attendance, so we contacted an old friend and longtime supporter, the Reverend Joseph Darby, the presiding elder of the AME churches in a nearby district. Reverend Darby advised us on how to arrange with Emanuel's interim pastor for me to go in quietly and without notice. Reverend Darby understood why I wanted to be there without my having to tell him. This congregation was hurting and in need, and I knew my showing up so soon after my son's death could be some source of strength for the Emanuel family. I also knew it would give me a sense of solace to be of comfort to these people in pain. The act of consoling had always made me feel a little better, and I was hungry to feel better.

More than that, I think, I really wanted to feel the extraordinary embrace of Emanuel AME Church and its parishioners. I was in need of their strength. I was in need of their grace. Read about the history of that church and the aftermath of its awful new tragedy and you will understand why. Mother Emanuel had been a haven for its flock and a bulwark against the predations of slavery and racial discrimination for nearly two hundred years. The church was struggling to keep hold of the younger community, and losing membership in 2015, but it had not lost its way. The people of Emanuel I had read about, and the parishioners I had met at the memorial a couple of days earlier, seemed free of the emotional scar tissue of bitterness and cynicism one would have expected from people who had been struggling so long against others who were determined to hate them. I had been awestruck by their capacity for forgiveness, even for a murderer who remorselessly shot and killed nine of their best and most beloved. The daughter of one of the victims had gone to the bond hearing to talk to her mother's killer. "I will never talk to her ever again. I will never be able to hold her again," Nadine Collier said of her mother, as the gunman stared blankly. "But I forgive you and have mercy on your soul. You hurt me. You hurt a lot of people. But God forgives you. And I forgive you."

The mother of the youngest victim was having a harder time with forgiveness. Felicia Sanders had been there in the room, cowering in fear, and heard her son's last words. "You don't have to do this," he had said to the killer. "We mean you no harm."

"I have to do this," the gunman said, before he shot Felicia's twenty-six-year-old son. "I have to finish my mission."

Felicia Sanders admitted to struggling. "With me, forgiveness is a process," she would say. "Sometimes I have to have a prodding from God to forgive people for small things. When it comes to something this magnificent, it would be a whole process for me." There was an incredible grace, to me, in her effort.

Hunter wanted to come with me, so we drove over that Sunday morning and pinned EMANUEL 9 ribbons onto our lapels on the way into the church. Emanuel was overflowing that day, and when the pastor who had replaced Reverend Pinckney, Norvel Goff Sr., called on all visitors to stand, I was surprised by how many worshippers got up on their feet. People from all over the country had come to share fellowship and show support to that church family. There were as many white visitors as black at the church that morning. The shooter had not incited a race war; quite the opposite: he had incited an incredible outpouring of support for Emanuel among both whites and blacks.

Reverend Goff asked me to say a few words that morning. "I wish I could say something that would ease the pain of the families and of the church," I told them. "But I know from experience, and I was reminded of it again twenty-nine days ago, that no words can mend a broken heart. No music can fill the gaping void. . . . And sometimes, as all preachers in here know, sometimes even faith leaves you just for a second. Sometimes you doubt. . . . There's a famous expression that says faith sees best in the dark, and for the nine families, this is a very dark, dark time."

I had not planned to make any sort of speech, but I had made some notes just in case, and was ready with a psalm that had given me comfort:

Your love, Lord, reaches to the heavens,
    your faithfulness to the skies.
Your righteousness is like the highest
    mountains, your justice like the great
    deep.
You, Lord, preserve both people and
    animals.
How priceless is your unfailing love, O God!

> People take refuge in the shadow of your
> wings.

"I pray, I pray that the families will find refuge in the shadow of His wings, and I pray that the love that all of you have shown to them, and people around the country to me, will help mend the broken hearts of their families and mine."

When the service was done Reverend Goff, Reverend Darby and his wife, and Charleston's mayor, Joe Riley, wanted to take me on a brief tour. The sun was high and bright against the white church front when we got outside, sparkling down on a memorial display festooned with flowers and notes people had dropped off in the days after the shooting. We spent some time out front, looking at the still pageant of sympathy. I was about to leave when Mayor Riley grabbed me and said there was something else he wanted me to see, and he guided us all around the side and into the lower entrance of the church, down six steps and toward Clementa Pinckney's office. The reverend's wife and his six-year-old daughter had hidden in that office during the massacre. To the right and fifteen or twenty feet away I could see the large fellowship hall where the Bible study group met. Nine good people had been killed on this floor, right beneath the pews, just eleven days earlier, but this parish persevered. Church members had filled in the bullet holes with putty and continued the regular Wednesday night Bible study without missing a single week. One hundred and fifty people showed up for the Bible class the first Wednesday after the massacre. "This territory belongs to God," Reverend Goff had told the world.

I could feel emotion rising in my throat as I walked by. I had an overwhelming sense of gratitude for the people of Emanuel and all the people who had come to support them or sent money and prayers. I was convinced the show of public support for Emanuel was emboldening political leaders in South Carolina to step up and match their bravery and humanity. I really did believe that some good could come from this tragedy, and was heartened to see that politicians on both sides of the aisle in the state legislature were already talking about removing from their capitol grounds one of the most hurtful symbols to black southern-ers — the Confederate flag. "I found myself trying to defend the Confederate flag," Republican state senator Paul Thurmond, son of the onetime arch-segregationist Strom Thurmond, had said. "How do you defend it? I flat-out couldn't."

Mayor Riley kept me moving, right into Reverend Pinckney's office. On Pinckney's wall, right where he had put it, was a picture that brought me up short. It was a photograph of the reverend and me together, seven months earlier, when he had helped organize an event to rally local clergy right before the 2014 midterm elections. We were both smiling that day. Clementa Pinckney had so much ahead of him that last time we were together. Now he was gone.

I was up early the next morning and decided to go out for a bike ride on the hard sand beach. The weather was nearly perfect, as it had been for our entire trip to South Carolina — scattered clouds appeared on occasion but passed on the wind. There was a gentle breeze on my face as I rode up the beach, beyond the line of private houses, then beyond the Ocean Course Clubhouse and all the way to the end of the good riding, where the sand softened up and the tree line began to press nearer the water. The Secret Service agents were well back, trailing me in their dune buggies. Nobody else was around. And suddenly I remembered riding out to this very spot with Beau the last time he was down here with us.

"Dad," he had said that day. "Let's stop and sit down here." And so we sat, the two of us, just breathing it in. "Look, Dad, isn't it magnificent?" he had said. "Isn't it beautiful?"

And it was like I could hear him talking to me again. *Dad, let's stop and sit down.* I got off my bike and found myself standing at what felt like the edge of the earth — just ocean and beach and woodlands. It was magnificent. I found myself suddenly overwhelmed. I could feel my throat constrict. My breath came shorter and shorter. I turned my back to the agents, looked out at the vastness of the ocean to one side and the darkness of the woods to the other, sat down on the sand, and sobbed.

CHAPTER ELEVEN:
RUN, JOE, RUN

A story ran in the *Wall Street Journal* on our last day in South Carolina. WILL HE RUN? the headline read. BIDEN SPECULATION MOUNTS. "It's no secret that Beau wanted him to run," was how the *Journal* quoted one of my longtime friends and political supporters. "If he does what Beau wanted him to do, he'll run." The story didn't get much traction in the press, for which I was grateful, because I was really struggling. In the immediate aftermath of Beau's passing, just thinking about running for president was beyond me. "Everything we talked about is over," I had said to my chief of staff, Steve Ricchetti, who had been overseeing my campaign planning along with Mike Donilon.

Running for the Democratic nomination was all tied up with Beau. Was all tied up with the entire family. Before he got sick, Beau felt strongly that I should run, as did

306

Hunt. Jill and Ashley had been very supportive. We all knew how much was at stake for the country, and we all believed I was best equipped to finish the job Barack and I had started. If Beau had never gotten sick, we would already be running. This was something we would have done together, with enthusiasm. *Remember, Dad,* Beau would be saying. *Home base. Home base.* The thought of doing it without him was painful. But as the days passed, the idea of not running started to feel like letting him down, like letting everybody down. Hunt still thought the race would give us purpose — something big to focus on that would help us deal with our profound sorrow. Jill thought we should continue to consider the possibility. I sometimes reflected on the courage Beau showed in his battle with an almost certainly unbeatable foe. "Beau lost his fight," one of the doctors at Anderson had said, "but he was never defeated." I wanted to be able to summon the courage to live up to Beau's example. But I wasn't sure if I would be able to find the emotional energy, and I knew from previous experience that grief is a process that respects no schedule and no timetable. I would be ready when I was ready, *if* I was ready, and not before. I had no idea when that would be.

But I also knew that if there was any chance for me to run, the complicated mechanics of mounting a campaign had to be considered. So I asked Mike and Steve to take some time outside of their regular day jobs to do a serious analysis. Was there still a path? Could we actually have a campaign ready in time to win? It didn't take them much time to restart the process. The truth is, we had begun talking seriously about the 2016 presidential race in the summer of 2013. When Steve dropped me off at the train station for the August vacation that year, we had already developed a message and a game plan we were going to begin to execute. But just a few days later Jill and I and the entire family had found ourselves at the M. D. Anderson Cancer Center absorbing the news of Beau's diagnosis, and we had put everything on hold.

Now Mike and Steve got to work quickly, and by the second week of July, after conferring with other advisers, they had made a serious assessment of the current state of the race and whether there was still an opening for me. We had a series of meetings in the few blank spaces in my official calendar over three days to discuss whether or not it was even plausible. The group was my most trusted circle only: Jill, Hunter, and Ashley; my sister Val; my longtime friend and chief of staff in my early Senate days, Ted Kaufman; Steve and Mike. The consensus was that the race was still wide open, and if we did well in the early states we could compete all the way to the end and had a good chance of winning the nomination. We thought there was enough time to put together the money and the ground game to compete in the four early states: Iowa, New Hampshire, Nevada, and South Carolina. And if we did as well as we hoped, we knew there would be no problem raising money for the rest of the campaign. Somebody pointed out that defeat, especially a big defeat of a sitting vice president, would be a real hit to my legacy. "There's no romantic dignity in losing," they said. "Understand, if you lose, it will be a big loss."

I just took it in. I understood the difference between an electoral loss and real loss. I wasn't afraid of losing a political race. And I believed that if I could muster the courage to run I'd be the best-qualified, most capable person in the field. The instinct in the room was to keep alive the possibility of a run.

My small team got to work on the nuts and bolts of a presidential campaign: field staff, fund-raising, and message. Greg Schultz, who had run Ohio for Obama-Biden and knew the best organizers around the country, volunteered to put together a field operation; and Michael Schrum, the former deputy national finance director at the DNC, volunteered to organize a staff to develop a fund-raising plan. Mike Donilon already had a clear idea of what the message should be — it wasn't fundamentally different from the message we had developed two years earlier — and he was going to turn it into an announcement speech. It would also function as the mission statement: here is why I am running and here is why I believe in the mission so deeply. "If you can't write a good announcement speech," somebody said, "you shouldn't run."

I think we all emerged from those meetings with a belief that we still had enough time and that we needed to be moving forward. But it didn't take me long to realize how far away I was from being emotionally ready for a presidential campaign, and how hard the decision to run was going to be. I flew out west on July 21 to speak at a pair of Democratic party fund-raisers, and when we touched down at Buckley Air Force Base in Aurora, Colorado, there was a group of military personnel and their families waving hello in the distance. They were about seventy yards away, so I jogged over to greet them. "Thank you," I said. "Thank you for your service." As I was shaking hands, I heard a voice in the back say, "Major Beau Biden, sir! Iraq, sir! Served with him, sir! Good soldier, sir! Good man!" I felt a lump rise in my throat. My breathing suddenly became shallower and my voice cracked. I was afraid I would be overwhelmed by emotion, and I think the audience could see it. I waved and hustled over to the car. This was no way for a presidential candidate to act in public.

Six days later I flew to Rochester, New York, to join Governor Andrew Cuomo in announcing a new investment in cutting-edge technology that could be used for alternative energy, medicine, construction, and manufacturing. And then I went to New York City to stand with him as he announced his extensive plans to remake La-Guardia Airport. I spent five hours that day with Andrew Cuomo, and the visit ended up being more personal than political. He understood the decision I was wrestling with, because he had seen his father, Governor Mario Cuomo, struggle over his decision about whether to run for president.

Mario had died earlier that year, so he was much on Andrew's mind. Andrew had also known Beau well; he had been elected attorney general of New York the same day Beau had been elected attorney general of Delaware. They had worked together and become friends. Andrew told me he and Beau used to commiserate about being aspiring politicians who were also the sons of well-known officeholders. They were both proud of us, proud to be our sons, but they agreed it made it hard to cut their own path. He told me they used to laugh about trying to "manage" their fathers, and joked about how demanding we could be, especially about our speeches. "My father always sought perfection," Andrew told me that day. "If it wasn't perfect — if the speech couldn't sing — he didn't want to give it. No matter what it was. If he was going to go out and speak to thirty people it mattered to him. And Beau said you were the same way."

I had always felt a kinship with Mario Cuomo. When I heard him give his celebrated speech at the 1984 Democratic National Convention, I remember thinking how much of his sense of fairness and justice and his disdain for those who abused their power flowed, like mine, from the teachings of the Catholic Church. I had told his family at his wake in January, and I had said it before in public, that Mario Cuomo was one of the few officeholders who I ever looked at and thought, whoa, this guy might be better than me.

And I had a growing appreciation for the difficulty of Mario's deliberations about running for president; no matter what the outside world was saying, for or against, the final decision had to feel right for him. Just as my decision would have to feel right for me. What Andrew did express to me that day at the end of July was that his father never truly made peace with declining to seek the presidency. "Whatever decision you make, make sure you won't regret it," he told me. "Because you'll live with it the rest of your life."

"Vice President Joseph R. Biden Jr. and his associates have begun to actively explore a possible presidential campaign, which would upend the Democratic field and deliver a direct threat to Hillary Rodham Clinton, several people who have spoken to Mr. Biden or his closest advisers say," read the lead of the front-page story on the *New York Times* on August 2. The news story relied on a column published the same day by the paper's own Maureen Dowd, who accurately reported that Beau had urged me to run. But the front-page news story, unlike Maureen, inaccurately portrayed this as a deathbed scene, with Beau speaking to me as he "lay dying." (They formally corrected it, but only months later.) The calls from outsiders, both in favor of my running and against, multiplied in the following days.

A few days after the story ran, Mike brought me a polished new draft of the announcement speech we had written, and it was all there in twenty-five hundred words — the mission statement. This would be a campaign based on one very basic principle: "We're one America," it read, "bound together in this great experiment of equality and opportunity and democracy. And everyone — and I mean everyone — is in on the deal."

We had to speak to those who felt left behind. They had to know we got their despair. It never ceased to amaze me the reaction I got when I would tell audiences that the longest walk a parent ever had to make was up a short flight of stairs to tell their son or daughter they were going to have to move because they couldn't find work or the bank was taking the house. I would tell them how my dad made that awful walk, and to just think of how many people had been forced to do the same in recent years. Tears would well up in so many eyes. It was real. They were living it.

We also had to speak to folks who were doing well. I took a lot of ridicule for saying rich folks were just as patriotic as anyone else. But I meant it. I had no doubt that most wealthy Americans were willing to forgo one more tax break in order to better educate our children, or to rebuild this nation's infrastructure, or to provide decent health care to everybody who needs it. They know that the opportunity to get richer isn't the whole deal. Lifting up their country is part of the deal, too.

We had to remind corporate America and Wall Street that just taking care of themselves and their shareholders wasn't good enough. They had a responsibility to their workers, their communities, and their country, too. Not to shame them, not to harangue them, but to remind them that a long history of shared prosperity and a secure and growing middle class is why America has had the most stable political democracy in the world. If we lose that — and we were losing it — no amount of money will hold back the anger and the pitchforks. This wasn't just about profits and economics.

This was about the social stability of this nation.

And most of all, we had to speak to the great middle class of the nation. And not just to their concerns, but to their aspirations, too. Revitalizing the hopes of the middle class — not shrinking them — was what this campaign was all about.

To speak to the middle class, I felt we had to do one more thing: Biden for President was going to reject the super PAC system. It was tempting to play the game because we would be getting such a late start. And for the first time in all my years of campaigning, I knew there was big money out there for me. But I also knew people were sick of it all. "We the People" didn't ring so true anymore. It was more like "We the Donors." And everybody understood that in a system awash with money, the middle class didn't have a fighting chance. Rejecting super PAC money wasn't a hardship for me. It felt like coming full circle. One of the very first bills I wrote as a United States senator was for public funding of elections. Now, foolhardy or not, I was going to try to upend the new money rush that was overwhelming our politics.

I was sure this message would stand out, because the campaign I was witnessing in the summer of 2015 was so negative, so dreary, so divisive, so personal. So *small.* I didn't buy the woe-is-me attitude about our national prospects that was being peddled by the other candidates. We had come through so much as a nation, and we were heading in the right direction. The country had dug out of an incredible hole in the previous six years, thanks to President Obama. Our administration had helped to create thirteen million new jobs and over-seen a record sixty-seven straight months of private-sector job creation. The nation's deficit had been cut in half. And we were finally moving from recovery to resurgence; the country was poised to take off.

I was proud to have worked alongside the president throughout it all and proud to run on our record — without apology, or reser-vation, or retreat. And as I would tell anyone who asked I was happy to shoulder the blame for anything we got wrong — just as long as they were willing to give me at least some of the credit for what we got right. And now, we were at a turning point. Now we were in a position where we could move from what we had to do to what we wanted to do.

That made the prospect of a presidential campaign exciting — and liberating. Starting so late, with no money, with all the "smart" people writing me off — I knew what I was up against. Which meant a cautious, trim-around-the-edges campaign was pointless. So Biden for President was going to go big. Because frankly, at this point in my career and after all my family had been through, anything less just wasn't worth it. We were going to go after a tax system that had lost all fairness and made no sense. We were going to get rid of the trust fund tax break and the "carried interest" giveaway to hedge fund managers. We were going to put an end to taxing earned income more heavily than unearned income, because I didn't see why people who invested for a living were being treated better than people who worked for a living. And we were going after the mountain of loopholes that had built up over the years. We had gone from having $600 billion worth of so-called tax expenditures (i.e., loopholes) in the federal budget when Ronald Reagan was president to more than $1.3 trillion today. No one could tell me they all made sense.

That's why I'd long thought that when people would tell me we didn't have the money to handle our problems, it was just nonsense. Just getting rid of the trust fund tax break could pay for free community college tuition. Just that alone.

A fifteen-dollar minimum wage. Free tuition at our public colleges and universities. Real job training. On-site affordable child care. Equal pay for women. Strengthening the Affordable Care Act. A job creation program built on investing in and modernizing our roads and bridges and our water and sewer systems. A middle-class tax cut. These were all within our power. It was a question of will.

So many of the presidential campaigns that summer seemed locked in the past. A fight over what happened, what went wrong, what America had lost. If I ran, I wanted to paint a picture of America's future, what we could become, how everyone could be dealt back into the deal. We needed what I called an American Renewal Project. That wasn't just about our needs — it was about our spirit, too. We didn't just want an infrastructure bill with money for highways, railroads, and airports. We were going to fund the highways of tomorrow, with thousands of charging stations for electric cars and dedicated lanes for self-driving cars. Those lanes could cut travel time in rush-hour Los Angeles in half. We wanted bullet trains capable of traveling more than 220 miles an hour; jets that could fly from coast to coast

319

in an hour or two. Because that was the future. I had fought to create a smart grid for America's electricity when we put together the Recovery Act. I was certainly going to fight for it as president. I was also going to fight for better gun safety. We had to overcome the cowardice and stand up to the NRA. New technologies such as hand recognition gun technology might just prevent another Newtown or Charleston. We wouldn't just provide extra funding for cancer research; we would create and fund a Cancer Moonshot to reinvent the systems for prevention, research, and care, bringing together the best clinicians, scientists, and other experts to double the rate of progress and deliver real outcomes for patients. Why couldn't we end cancer as we know it?

Mike was more bullish than ever about the run. In early August, he presented the case that I was in better shape as a candidate now than I had been six months earlier; my poll numbers were up, and still on the rise. My favorable ratings were higher than those of any candidate in the race — in either party. My numbers on trustworthiness, honesty, and empathy were as high as they had ever been. And I was strongest where the most formidable candidate, Hillary

Clinton, was weakest: the key swing states like Pennsylvania, Ohio, and Florida. The president must have been getting an earful from his political team — a few of whom were actively working for Hillary's nomination — because at our next lunch he again asked me straight up what I was planning. "Mr. President," I said, "I'm not ready to make up my mind." I was still working through whether I was prepared to give it all of my energy for the next year and a half. "I'm taking it one day at a time. If we do decide to go, we'll decide in time to be viable." The president was not encouraging.

A lot happening, I wrote in my diary when I finally got some downtime in Wilmington the next weekend. *Need to be careful it doesn't get away from me. I need to slow down, ramp down, my schedule for the month of August. I've got to figure out what I need to know to be ready.*

I was assiduous about keeping my own deliberations within the trusted circle, but I was getting plenty of outside advice. The chatter among Democratic Party insiders and most of the political pundit class was that it was too late. I could not raise the money. There was no good talent left out there to fill up a real campaign structure and staff a viable ground game, and once I got in the race all my wonderful poll numbers would collapse. A lot of people were telling us that my high favorability ratings were merely temporary — the function of the public sympathy surrounding Beau's death. A *Politico* reporter covering one of Hillary's fundraisers on Martha's Vineyard, where Barack was also seen playing a round of golf with Bill Clinton, made my quixotic effort the lead of the story. "As Joe Biden considers a possible run for president," the *Politico* reporter noted on August 16, "the donors he'd need to be viable appear to be ruling him out. . . ."

"There really is no contest right now," said one donor. "I think people are unifying around Hillary."

A couple of people on President Obama's political team were telling us the race just wasn't winnable for me. There was usually a preamble: *We're very protective of the vice president. We don't want to see Joe get hurt. We can only imagine what he's going through right now.* But they were not subtle. They asked Steve and Mike to consider the incredible historical forces around Barack Obama in 2008, when he ran against the Clinton machine and still just barely won. And if she almost beat us, they implied, she will definitely beat you. I heard it all and understood the difficulties, but none of that much mattered. Just as it didn't matter how fast the Bernie Sanders movement was building or how vulnerable Hillary suddenly looked. The other candidates simply weren't my main consideration.

I spent a full week of the August vacation at our house in Wilmington, refining the announcement speech and trying to breathe myself back into my old life. We didn't get to spend much time at our house on the lake anymore, so it felt good to work the property. I got out the chain saw and took down some dead trees, replaced failing lightbulbs, power-washed the stucco walls. I had to call a contractor to get an estimate for installing a new tin roof on the tiny outbuilding by the lake where we kept the fishing poles.

There were a lot of calls coming in from people encouraging me to run, especially from former colleagues in the Senate: Don Riegle, Bob Kerrey, Chris Dodd, Tom Daschle, who had told me months earlier that if I decided to go he was in 100 percent. Bill Bradley must have had me on speed dial. Gary Hart weighed in. So did Kent Conrad. "Joe has a humanity about him that comes across," the former senator from

North Dakota said publicly. "He is for real. He believes in things. He is able to articulate his values, and I think he would acquit himself extremely well." The former governor of Iowa, Chet Culver, called to say the state was wide open and he was ready to help. The former chairman of the South Carolina Democratic Party, Dick Harpootlian, was urging me to get in the race. "The country needs Joe Biden," he was saying in public. And my best political operative in South Carolina, Trip King, had a list of serious supporters, including Charleston mayor Joe Riley and, by his count, more than half of the twenty-three members of the black caucus in the state legislature. Some of Obama's top fund-raisers called to sign on, like Azita Raji, the nominee to be ambassador to Sweden, who offered to stay home and be my national finance chairman instead. And Denise Bauer, who said she was willing to leave her job as ambassador to Belgium to come home and help me. There were dozens of others, including mayors, state legislators, fund-raisers, and Democratic campaign consultants. I promised to keep all these calls and offers confidential. I didn't want to leave anybody out on a limb in case I decided I wasn't able to run. I didn't want their loyalty to me to jeopardize their relationship with another candidate.

There were a few different kinds of messages being sent my way through the press. "I just want the vice president to do what's right for him and his family," Hillary said at a campaign stop in Iowa. "I have a great deal of admiration and affection for him. I think he has to make what is a very difficult decision for himself and his family. He should have the space and opportunity to decide what he wants to do." But by then the opposition research had already started on me. There was a big story at the end of August about the community policing crime bill that I had authored and Bill Clinton had heralded as a great step forward when he signed it as president in 1994. He was now calling it a big mistake. That was followed by a story alleging I was cozy with the banking and credit card industry when I was a senator. And Clinton backers sent the signal that they would not stop at voting records and policies if I did get in the race. "There's not a whole lot of daylight on issues, that's the problem," one of her supporters told a reporter from *Politico.* "The attack would be on his aptitude to be president, and that's going to be a very tough thing to do."

I focused on the calls of support, which

meant a lot to me — especially coming from people who had known and served with me over the years. This support would make a difference if I ran, but it didn't make the decision any easier. The real issue, the crux of the matter, was brought home during that full week in Wilmington in August. Beau's children, Hunter and Natalie, were just a five-minute drive away, so they spent a lot of time at our house. Hunter could hop on a little plastic skiff and paddle diagonally across the lake, from the dock to the far end, 150 yards away, then go exploring in the woods and emerge with a newly captured turtle. Natalie spent most of her time at the pool. The best times were when we were all together at the pool, down below the back porch and the sunroom, splashing around in the water or lolling in the sun. "Pop," Natalie would say sometimes, "I see Daddy all the time." Hunter would lie down on my chest, out in the sun, and fall asleep. "You smell like Daddy," he said one afternoon, with his head on my chest. "You're not going to leave me, are you, Pop?"

I thought the decision was going to be simple after that; my grief had its own specific weight, and it was not feeling any lighter at the end of August. I knew also, from hard-earned experience, that the second year is in some ways the hardest. The shock is over, as is the strangeness of living through all the first holidays and anniversaries and birthdays, and the undeniable permanence of the loss begins to settle in. If I did win the nomination the next summer, we would all be trying to deal with that new layer of grief in the middle of a general election.

The thing to do would be to get out now, while all those people who were sticking by me had a chance to go claim their places in another campaign. But I kept hearing Beau. *Promise me, Dad. Promise me you're going to be okay.* Jill was not pushing me to run, but she didn't want me to make my choice until I was *sure.* She understood exactly what I was going through, how much I was hurting, because she was going through it, too. She kept saying, "Keep your shoulders back, Joe. Keep your shoulders back. Smile when you talk about Beau." Steve and Mike were telling me to just give it a little more time, that my resilience was what was going to set me apart.

And on Labor Day, out in the open air, at a parade in downtown Pittsburgh, it felt as if something was happening. I was surprised by the reception I received. So were Leo

Gerard, the president of the steelworkers union, and Rich Trumka, the head of the AFL-CIO, who were both there with me. The response was overwhelming. Thousands of people lined the street. A thousand or more marched. It was a big, loud, excited crowd. Young, old, white, black, Hispanic. An eight-year-old boy in a Superman T-shirt. Teenage girls in bright-colored headbands. Working moms with WOMEN OF STEEL shirts. Middle-aged men with their grandchildren on their shoulders. There were skateboards, bikes, and wheelchairs. It felt like America. There were chants of "Run, Joe, Run!" People holding up hand-lettered BIDEN FOR PRESIDENT signs. I think the enthusiasm caught the press off guard as well. I felt like I was back in my old form. This was the first physical manifestation of the momentum I had felt building for the last six weeks. There were too many people to greet them all, but I tried to get to as many as I could. I found myself jogging, faster and faster, zigzagging from one side of the avenue to the other, chest out and shoulders back, trying to get to more people as I went. It was hot, but I felt alive. It felt good. Really good.

ABC World News Tonight led its broadcast with me that night. "A fired-up Joe

Biden . . . Is this a man in the running?" And things just started to roll from there. Three days later I was a featured guest on the first week of the new *Late Show with Stephen Colbert*. Colbert let me talk a lot in the first segment about Beau and what my son meant to me. It was a good test. I thought I did pretty well, without getting too emotional. Maybe I was turning a corner. By the time we came back from the commercial break, his crowd was chanting, "Joe! Joe! Joe! Joe!"

"Do you have anything to tell us about your plans?" he asked.

"Look, I don't think any man or woman should run for president unless, number one, they know exactly why they would want to be president; two, they can look at the folks out there and say, 'I promise you, you have my whole heart, my whole soul, my energy, and my passion, to do this.' And I'd be lying if I said that I knew I was there. I'm being completely honest. Nobody has a right, in my view, to seek that office unless they're willing to give it 110 percent of who they are. I'm optimistic, I'm positive about where we're going, but I find myself . . ." I started to get emotional again. "Sometimes," I finally continued, "it just overwhelms you." And I found myself telling him the story about the air base in Denver where I got choked up.

When I got off the set I was relieved that I had held it together, but I was drained. Hunter saw how hard it was. "Dad, you were great," he said to me when I got home, "but we've got to stop talking about the loss of Beau. We have to talk about all that Beau accomplished and we have to talk about the future."

The reviews of the *Colbert* interview the next day put talk of Biden for President into overdrive. "It was an extremely rare sighting given our culture and our politics today," Mike Barnicle said at the top of *Morning Joe.* "It was an actual human being." I was still in New York that day to help Governor Cuomo mark the anniversary of September 11. Andrew had already endorsed his home state's former senator Hillary Clinton for president, but he was still pushing me to think hard about running. *Don't make a decision you'll regret.* And he was effusive in his praise for me. "Today is about human beings and character," he told a meeting of first responders. "This is a man who is authentic. This is a man who is genuine. . . . When he's with you, he looks you in the eye and tells you he's with you. . . . He's all heart. He's here to do the right thing. He's a friend in good days and bad days."

Four days later the conservative *New York Times* columnist David Brooks wrote that my appearance on *Colbert* had changed his mind. He now believed I should run. "Every presidential candidate needs a narrative to explain how his or her character was formed," he wrote. "With Stephen Colbert he revealed a story and suggested a campaign that is moving, compelling and in tune with the moment." Two days after that, on the trip that put me over the million-mile mark for official travel as vice president, the mayor of Los Angeles leaned on me to run. Even more surprising, an executive in the entertainment industry insisted that I had more support in the Hollywood community than Hillary. He said I could raise money there without a problem. George Clooney got in touch with Steve Ricchetti soon after that. "I love Joe Biden," he told my chief of staff, "and if he decides to do this I will step up with any and all assistance I can provide. I think I've proved I'm a pretty good fund-raiser, so that's all anyone asks me to do. But I am invested in this. I am willing to take a campaign role if you want me."

Mike kept saying the good feelings about me were not dissipating; in fact, my character numbers were getting better. As a matter of politics — my personal traits, my message, my history — the case for my candidacy was growing stronger, he said. Authenticity mattered more and more to voters. The need in the field for somebody to speak to the middle class was more urgent and the call for somebody who could work across partisan divides more insistent. Mike believed even more strongly in September than he did in July that I could win.

Bill Bradley called, again, when I got back from California. This was my time, he insisted. He told me about a woman he'd overheard in a coffee shop saying I ought to run. "And I do not want to see him attacked," she had said to a friend. "He has been through too much."

"Joe, sometimes the man meets the moment," my old colleague told me. "Tragedy has bonded you to the public, and you can build on that. Joe, this is your moment. You'll take the entire country with you if you stand up." He told me he wasn't trying to pressure me, that I should take my time and be sure I was ready for this. It wasn't too late, he said, if that woman in the coffee shop was right. "You're a special case."

I knew it would be an uphill race against

Hillary, but I thought I could win. It had to have been very tough for her to make the decision to run, because she knew her detractors would come after her. And they did. Her numbers, in the face of relentless attacks by Republicans and critical press coverage, were declining. Bernie Sanders was polling eleven points ahead of her in New Hampshire and had closed to a tie in Iowa. She was unable to shake the focus on her emails and the speaking fees from Wall Street. I wasn't sure how much it mattered, but I was running stronger than her in head-to-head matchups against the Republicans in the field. "For a guy who is not running for president," said the director of Monmouth University Polling Institute, "Biden sure is making headway against the front-runner." The firefighters' union had decided to withhold their endorsement of her until I made up my mind. The head of the AFL-CIO was saying nice things about me, which was causing great consternation at Hillary's headquarters. It was clear the Clinton campaign was very worried about my entering the race.

A sharp new dynamic was rising. Steve and Mike had been getting calls for months from close friends in the Clinton campaign and people they had worked with on President Obama's team. They tended to be fishing expeditions. *So what are you guys up to? This isn't for real, is it?* But there was a new edge to the calls. The Clinton camp had started to rethink the old narrative they were pitching about my self-destructive, quixotic errand. Now they were saying that if I ran I was going to be such a powerful force that I would split the party in half, or take so many votes from Hillary that Bernie would waltz off with the nomination. Then the general election would be lost for sure. A few close advisers to Obama were still telling Steve and Mike we couldn't win. *Why don't you get it?*

The truth was, I was comfortable, as was the rest of the team, with our underdog status this early in the race. The increasing pushback made everybody a little bit angry and a lot determined. Steve made the case to anybody in the building who would listen that I had earned the right to make my own decision. And that no one should prejudge the race for the Democratic nomination before the first vote was cast. I could tell the people on my own team were starting to get their game faces on by the beginning of October.

We called a meeting for October 5 to make a final judgment on whether or not we could put a first-rate team on the ground and raise the necessary money. Steve and Mike were there along with Greg Schultz and Michael Schrum, who had both been working on the nuts and bolts since July. Jill, Val, and Hunter were there. And Ted Kaufman. But the circle had widened now and included people like Bob Bauer and Anita Dunn, who had been key players on the Obama team. Bob, who had been White House legal counsel, had worked out an understanding with his firm that made it possible for him on his own time to act as one of my key personal advisers as I worked through this decision. I sat, almost stunned, as they talked through mechanics. It was clear we had the time to meet all the state filing deadlines. We knew exactly how much money we would need to compete in the first four states and we had the means to raise it — even with our decision not to take advantage of super PACs that could receive unlimited donations from wealthy individuals. We had commitments from more than fifty specific individuals, each with a track record of raising a minimum of $250,000 for Obama-Biden, who were all willing to do it again for Biden 2016. We just had to ask.

Greg Schultz had identified state directors

in Iowa, New Hampshire, Nevada, and South Carolina. He had lined up the best organizers in swing states like Pennsylvania, Ohio, and Florida. It was clear there was plenty of talent left, and they were ready to get on board. Anita Dunn, Obama's former communications director, was already in the room. Pete Rouse, who had been Obama's deputy chief of staff, had agreed to join us too. I was really proud to see how many former members of President Obama's campaign team, his White House staff, and even members of his cabinet were willing to pitch in to help me.

We had put together an impressive list of endorsements. Anita had a media plan for an announcement in two weeks, or in three. We were ready to find office space in Wilmington for the headquarters. By the end of the meeting it was clear to everybody in the room that we had the ability to staff a first-rate field operation and the capacity to raise the money to get us through the first four contests. I hadn't been sure of any of that at the beginning of July, but I was certain of it on October 5. Only one thing could stop me now — and that was me.

The next day, October 6, a story in *Politico* really threw me. The staff didn't even want me to see the headline — EXCLUSIVE: BIDEN HIMSELF LEAKED WORD OF HIS SON'S DYING WISH. "Joe Biden has been making his 2016 deliberations all about his late son since August," the *Politico* story said. "Aug. 1, to be exact — the day renowned Hillary Clinton critic Maureen Dowd published a column that marked a turning point in the presidential speculation. . . . Biden had effectively placed an ad in *The New York Times*."

I should have seen this coming, I guess.

But the *Politico* story exceeded even my worst expectations of what the opposition was going to be like. The idea that I would use my son's death to political advantage was sickening. I didn't think anybody would believe the charge, but I could feel my anger rise. And I understood the danger of that, especially in my present emotional state. If this thing about Beau came up somewhere in my hearing, I was afraid I would not be able to control my rage. And I would say or do something I would regret.

What turned out to be our final campaign meeting ran late into the night on Tuesday, October 20. The staff was still going through the specifics of the rollout when I noticed Mike Donilon really watching me. Mike had known me for thirty years. He had been at my side as we developed our message for 2016, and he had pushed back hard at all the naysayers along the way. "Don't take this away from him," he would say. Mike later told me that looking at me that night, as it got to zero hour, he could see my jaw clenching tighter. The pain he read on my face was off the charts. Mike also knew that Jill would have supported the decision to go, but he thought he saw dread in her eyes. I caught him looking at me and gestured, *What is it, Mike?*

"I don't think you should do this," he said.

It was the first time he had spoken against my running in the two years we had been talking about it. I understood Mike wasn't speaking as a political strategist, because I knew how profoundly he believed in my candidacy and that he still believed, like I did, that we could win. He was speaking as a friend.

When I sent everybody home that night, it was time for me to decide — and I did. The first person I told was Jill, then Hunter and Ashley.

I got up the next morning and called President Obama to let him know. Then I called Steve and Mike. Steve got on the phone with the White House chief of staff, who told him that the president had already said he would do whatever he could to help me. Barack made the generous offer to stand next to me when I made my announcement and invited us to come to the Rose Garden, behind the Oval Office, to do it there. Mike and Steve drove to the Naval Observatory early that morning and got in the car with me so we could spend the short ride to the White House talking about my remarks. "It's the right thing to do for the family," I told Mike on the way over. "It's the right thing to do for me."

The president had Jill and me into the Oval Office to review what I was going to say that morning; he could not have been more supportive. I knew I'd made the right decision when I walked into the Rose Garden with Jill on one side and Barack on the other to explain that I could not make the commitment required to run. Time had run out. The grieving process, I said, "doesn't respect or much care about things like filing deadlines or debates and primaries and caucuses." And I was still grieving.

I made sure to be upbeat, to keep my shoulders back, to smile. I had no prepared speech, just notes, but I knew I wanted to make it clear that I was still optimistic about the future of the country and that I was not going to stop speaking out. "I believe we have to end the divisive partisan politics that is ripping this country apart, and I think we can. It's mean-spirited. It's petty. And it's gone on for much too long. I don't believe, like some do, that it's naïve to talk to Republicans. I don't think we should look at Republicans as our enemies. They are our opposition, not our enemies. And for the sake of the country, we have to work together. . . . Four more years of this kind of pitched battle may be more than this country can take." And, almost as an afterthought, I said that I did have one regret. "If I could be anything," I said, "I would have wanted to have been the president that ended cancer, because it's possible."

Mike was there in the Rose Garden that day, just observing. "Joe Biden looked a little less pained," he would later say, "and a little less alive."

EPILOGUE

I was back in the air again on December 6, heading for Kyiv, adding to my million-plus miles traveled as vice president. I had been invited to address the members of Ukraine's parliament, the Rada, and I felt that this was as important a speech as I had ever made in Europe. Ukraine was at the crossroads of history at the end of 2015. I wanted to mark this moment, and to remind the men and women sitting in the Rada that they were on the cusp of something extraordinary and — like all the most worthwhile things in life — extraordinarily fragile. I had been working hard on the big themes of the speech for weeks, focusing not only on the language of the remarks but the tone I wanted to strike in delivering it. I was still emending the text as we flew east toward Europe.

At the front of my mind were the hundred or so Ukrainian civilians who had been killed almost two years earlier in the Revolution of Dignity protests in Kyiv — the "Heavenly Hundred," as they had come to be known. These Ukrainians were already enshrined as martyrs to the cause of liberty and independence, but they had been flesh and blood and bone, and had had reasons for hope and happiness, too. So I was also mindful of the very real pain suffered by a hundred families who had lost husbands, fathers, sons, wives, mothers, or daughters — and the thousands more who counted these people as dear and intimate friends. Those thousands of Ukrainians could still take solace in the possibility that the lives lost would be redeemed by a glorious new beginning for their country. *Amidst fire and ice, snipers on rooftops, the Heavenly Hundred paid the ultimate price of patriots the world over,* read the speech I was working through. *Their blood and courage delivering to the Ukrainian people a second chance for freedom. Their sacrifice — to put it bluntly — is now your obligation.*

Time was running out on the Ukrainian government to get it right. The country's economy was cracking, while Vladimir Putin continued applying force at all the weakest pressure points: the supplies of energy, the bond market, the venality long endemic in both business and politics in Ukraine. Corruption was strangling economic growth, hollowing out the military, and destroying trust in government. The Rada had created the new National Anti-Corruption Bureau and staffed it with detectives, but the new agency had not yet prosecuted anyone, and graft was still rampant in both the major political parties. The prosecutor general was himself reported to be tainted by corruption. Dedicated members of the reform movement were losing heart; one of its leaders wondered if Ukraine was about to crumble as a viable state. It appeared as likely as not that the sacrifice of the Heavenly Hundred — as well as the thousands of other Ukrainians who had died in the fighting since — would come to naught. That was what I was walking into in my first trip back to Ukraine since just before Thanksgiving a year earlier.

The flight path to eastern Europe that December took us over the North Atlantic, where, on a clear day, the first speck of land you see below is Ireland — which has been a defining touchstone in my own personal and family history. One of my colleagues in the Senate, Daniel Patrick Moynihan, once made this simple but profound observation about us Irish: "To fail to understand that life is going to knock you down is to fail to understand the Irishness of life." I knew the truth of it before I ever heard Senator Moynihan speak it aloud, as should any descendant of the Blewitts of County Mayo, where the River Moy begins to widen and lose itself into the North Atlantic, and the Finnegans of County Lough, on a volatile little inlet of the Irish Sea. I had been knocked down hard enough by then to understand the Irishness of life, and this past year had reminded me of it all over again.

But that was not the whole story of Irishness to me — not even the half of it. "Keep the faith, Joey," my grandfather Finnegan used to say to me when I walked out his door. "Remember, the best drop of blood in you is Irish." We Irish, I like to tell people, are the only people in the world who are actually nostalgic about the future. I have never stopped being a dreamer. I refuse to stop believing in possibilities. Flying over the North Atlantic on Air Force Two, working on that speech to the Rada, reminded me of all that, as it reminded me of another driving force in life — one I suspected I shared with all the elected officials in the Rada.

One thing I know from working with

politicians and national leaders across the world is that they are a lot more like me than unlike me. Most of us aspire to the same thing: the opportunity to be part of creating something truly consequential and meaningful for their country; the chance to be part of a historic moment and to be remembered for their courage and vision in having acted. So I believed I knew what kind of political sermon would move those Ukrainian legislators. When I was just barely a teenager, my mother asked me what I wanted to do, or be, when I grew up, and I only knew one thing for sure. I wanted to make a difference, to be part of some significant historical change. I guess it was because I was thinking about civil rights.

This drive is an undeniably powerful force, and I believe harnessing it in the service of something good is our best hope for the future. So as I prepared the speech, I understood I had to do a lot more than simply announce to the Ukrainian legislators an additional $190 million of direct aid from the United States; or to assure them that the U.S. and its allies were going to keep supporting them in the face of military and economic pressure from Putin and keep defending their right as a sovereign nation to make their own decisions and choose their own allies; or to remind them that they had to continue to root out the rampant corruption in their national politics. None of that would be enough for the job at hand. I felt I had to remind them of their higher purpose.

By the time I stepped to the podium in the Rada on December 7, I was determined to appeal to something beyond their immediate self-interest: the chance to bequeath to their children and grandchildren the freedom and democracy that had eluded them for centuries. So I told them they had arrived at a moment of being able to create a real, independent, and sustainable democracy in Ukraine that was akin to America's own revolutionary moment more than two hundred years earlier. "It began when men of conscience stood up in legislative bodies representing every region in what was then Colonial America — Massachusetts, Pennsylvania, Virginia, very different interests — and declared in each of their regions the inherent rights of free people . . . the inherent right to be free," I told them. "They took a vast continent and a diverse people — what John Adams, one of our Founding Fathers and future presidents, called 'an unwieldy machine' — and they molded that unwieldy machine into a united representative democracy where people saw themselves as Americans first and citizens of their region second." The accomplishment put Washington, Adams, Jefferson, Franklin, Madison, Hamilton, and dozens of others into the history books.

"You have a historic opportunity to be remembered as the Rada that finally and permanently laid in place the pillars of freedom that your people have longed for, yearned for, for so many years," I told the whole of Ukraine's elected body. "This is your moment. This is your responsibility." They had to put aside the partisan and parochial, and strive for what Edmund Burke called "the general good." If they succeeded, I really believed, their grandchildren would speak their names in hushed and reverent tones.

"This is all within your power," I told the members of the Rada. "It's within your hands. Nobody else's — yours."

Nobody ever told me a life in politics and public service would be easy; like life, I never expected politics to be free of disappointment or heartache. But I have always believed it was worth the effort. And having been in elective office and public service since I was twenty-seven years old, I had come to understand that all good things are hard and take time. It might take a generation or more to know if the Revolution of Dignity in Ukraine had truly succeeded. Just as it would take a generation or more to know if the U.S. investment in the Northern Triangle countries of Honduras, Guatemala, and El Salvador would really transform those places into safe and secure democratic nations with expanding economies and a thriving and well-educated middle class. Just as it would be a generation or more before we knew if all the blood and treasure spent — and all the effort expended by Beau and hundreds of thousands of other American troops in Iraq — would birth an inclusive and unified democracy based on freedom and religious tolerance. I was determined even in my last year in office to do what I could to keep things moving in the right direction. And they were.

About a week after my return from Kyiv, Congress approved a $750 million appropriation for the Northern Triangle countries that I had invested an enormous amount of my personal time and reputation achieving. It was triple the previous year's appropriation, and would be enough to begin helping political leaders in the Northern Triangle provide civil governments responsive to their respective citizens, as well as increased security and opportunity. And then, in the last week of December, with the assistance of United States military trainers and more than six hundred coalition air strikes carried out on ISIL targets, the Iraqi security forces won Ramadi back from the jihadists. Prime Minister Abadi's coalition of Shia and Sunni fighters had taken the city, and they held it. Abadi's commanders were already drawing up plans for clearing other key cities in Anbar and would eventually move on Mosul. It made me proud to know that when Abadi had called nine months earlier and said, "Joe, I need your help," I went to bat for him. And I think it made a difference.

President Obama had a surprise for me at his final State of the Union address, in January 2016. "Last year, Vice President Biden said that with a new moonshot, America can cure cancer," he said, about twenty-five minutes into the speech. "Tonight, I'm announcing a new national effort to get it done. And because he's gone to the mat for all of us, on so many issues over the past forty years, I'm putting Joe in charge of mission control. For the loved ones we've all lost, for the family we can still save, let's make America the country that cures cancer once and for all. What do you say, Joe?" I was receiving this news at the same time the rest of the country did. As the president turned to me and nodded, I looked out and saw former colleagues on both sides of the aisle on their feet, applauding. It gave me hope that we could do something significant.

Barack had seen what my family had gone through the last few years, not only the hard times, but the times when the genius and the effort of the medical team at M. D. Anderson had given us real hope. He had heard me in the White House Rose Garden a few months earlier when I spoke of my only real regret about not running: that I would not be the president who oversaw the end of cancer as we know it. When the president handed me mission control, every member of the federal bureaucracy knew that I had his full authority to martial all the assets within the government — as well as to reach out to the expert community nationally and internationally. This was the first time any president had delegated the authority to one individual to get the job done. He was handing me a remarkable opportunity — a chance to help save other families from what we had just gone through.

I have spent the past few years working to accelerate the fight against cancer. I believe we are on the cusp of real and significant breakthroughs, and I have dedicated myself to doing two things — bringing a sense of urgency to the fight and making sure the systems of prevention, research, and patient care are designed to take advantage of the best of twenty-first-century science and technology. We're on the verge of supercomputer capability that will provide a billion billion calculations per second — increasing our chances of finding new answers if we can bring together data from thousands, or millions, of patients. I have been encouraging a system that honors team science and increased collaboration and data sharing among clinicians, researchers, and medical experts at the different cancer centers across the nation and around the world. I have been working to make the best prevention and care available to all communities, so outcomes aren't wholly dictated by zip code, and helping to find ways to incentivize pharmaceutical companies to work with one another to provide for more combination therapies in clinical trials. At the heart of it all is my desire to encourage a system and a culture that put the interests of the patients and their families ahead of all other considerations. I learned first-hand, the hardest way possible, that facing down cancer is a frightening and costly ordeal in the best of circumstances, for the strongest of families. We need to identify any and all extra obstacles placed in front of these suffering people, mark these obstacles as inexcusable, and work to abolish them.

The effort has bipartisan support in Congress, help from businesses across the country, and commitments from many other countries to engage with us in the effort to end cancer as we know it. The goal is within our reach, and reaching that goal will remind us of something the country seems to have lost sight of: There is nothing we cannot accomplish as Americans if we set our minds to it. There is no challenge we cannot meet. I am more optimistic about our chances today than when I was elected to the Senate as a twenty-nine-year-old kid. The twenty-first century is going to be another American Century.

As I write this, in the summer of 2017, I still think of the question Barack put to me in his private dining room just off the Oval Office back in January 2015. "Joe," he had asked, "how do you want to spend the rest of your life?" The answer I gave him then still holds today. In fact, it was the same answer I would have given when I was making my start in public life. The same answer I would have given every time I ran for the United States Senate. The same answer I would have given when I left my thirty-six-year career in the Senate to become vice president. The same answer I would have given before Beau got his diagnosis, and all through his battle with cancer, and every day since. The difference now is that I have another voice in my head, both calming and insistent. *You've got to promise me, Dad, that no matter what happens, you're going to be all right. Give me your word, Dad. You're going to be all right.*

Beau had not been explicit that night at his dinner table, just weeks before our final Nantucket Thanksgiving together, when he asked me to make that promise. He didn't have to be. We could always finish each other's thoughts. Beau's meaning was clear. He was also counting on Hunt to be there to make sure I kept my promise. And I wear Beau's rosary around my wrist every day now, as I have since he passed, as a reminder of what he was expecting of me. I had to do my duty — for the duration. I had to do my

353

job as husband, father, and Pop. I had to pull my weight to help Hallie take care of the children, Natalie and Hunter. I had to be present for Jill and Hunt and Ashley. But family was not the main thing. Beau knew the family was built solid, that there was no tide strong enough to wash it away. He had faith that it would endure. There was so much more for me to do beyond the family, and he was worried I would retreat from my obligations to the wider world. Beau was insisting that I stay true to myself and to all the things I had worked for over the years. He was making me promise to stay engaged in the public life of the nation and the world. *Home base, Dad. Home base.*

So how do I want to spend the rest of my life? I want to spend as much time as I can with my family, *and* I want to help change the country and the world for the better. That duty does much more than give me purpose; it gives me something to hope for. It makes me nostalgic for the future.

ACKNOWLEDGMENTS

This story was not an easy one for me to tell. There were many days I found it difficult to go back and revisit this time period; and my memories of events were sometimes foggy. There were a number of people I counted on to help me with recall, with the reconstruction chronologies, and with encouragement.

Thank you for all this, and more, to Kathy Chung, Mark and Libby Gitenstein, Colin Kahl, Michael Carpenter, Juan Gonzalez, Jeffrey Prescott, and Tony Blinken.

To Steve Ricchetti, Mike Donilon, Danielle Carnival, Don Graves, and Bob Bauer.

To Kevin O'Connor and John Flynn.

Thank you to the extraordinary team at M. D. Anderson Cancer Center: Dr. W. K. Alfred Yung, Dr. Raymond Sawaya, Dr. David Ferson, Dr. Frederick Lang, Eva Lu Lee, Chris Hagerman, and Yolanda Hart.

Thank you also to the folks at CAA for

shepherding this book to a publisher — Richard Lovett, Craig Gering, Mollie Glick, and David Larabell; and to the folks at Flatiron Books for shepherding this book to the reader — Bob Miller, Colin Dickerman, Greg Villepique, and James Melia.

This book would not be possible without the extraordinary talent, patience, and hard work of Mark Zwonitzer. I cannot thank Mark enough.

And thank you to my daughter-in-law Hallie, my daughter Ashley, my son Hunter, my son-in-law Howard, and my brother Jimmy. Special thanks to my sister Valerie. And most especially, thank you, Jill.

ABOUT THE AUTHOR

Joe Biden represented Delaware for 36 years in the U.S. Senate before serving as 47th Vice President of the United States from 2009 to 2017. As the Vice President, Joe Biden addressed important issues facing the nation and represented America abroad, traveling over 1.2 million miles to more than 50 countries. He convened sessions of the President's Cabinet, led interagency efforts, and worked with Congress in his fight to raise the living standards of middle class Americans, reduce gun violence, address violence against women, and end cancer as we know it. Since leaving the White House, Vice President Biden continues his legacy of expanding opportunity for all with the creation of the Biden Foundation, the Penn Biden Center for Diplomacy and Global Engagement at the University of Pennsylvania, and the Biden Domestic Policy Institute at the University of Delaware. He is the author of *Promises to Keep: On Life and Politics.*

36.99